PRAISE FO

M000316814

"*Never Alone* is a reminder of the most comforting truth given to the human race. Through scripture and story, Dugan reminds us that God is not a God out there but a God with us and for us."

— NANCY & JOHN ORTBERG, renowned authors and communicators

"I've known Dugan approximately forever. What makes me so happy is that now all kinds of people get to discover what I've known for years: that Dugan is a wise, honest, creative person, and that he has a lot to teach us all about what it means to walk with God, when we feel his presence, and when we don't. I can't wait to share the book with so many people in my life."

— SHAUNA NIEQUIST, author of *Bread & Wine* and *Savor*

"*Never Alone* is such an engaging read. I began reading, could not put it down, and time just flew by. Every teenager, twenty-something, and next-generation minister must read this. Dugan addresses an epidemic faith crisis hitting teenagers and young adults across the nation with such empathy I'm convinced any reader will find them saying over and over again, *Yes! So true! Wow, I thought I was the only one.*"

— SHANE FARMER, senior pastor at Cherry Hills Community Church and former director of Student Impact at Willow Creek Community Church

PRAISE FOR **NEVER ALONE**

"*Never Alone* is a stone-sober look at following Jesus. This is what students need, an honest forecast of what they can expect ahead so they don't think they've lost their minds when they get there."

– KARL CLAUSON, speaker, radio host, and author of
Thrill: When Normal is Not Enough

"This isn't just an interesting, informative, entertaining and biblically based book, it is an important book. It speaks to an issue that rocks teens in their faith: emotions. Dugan understands teens, loves Jesus, and speaks with passion and compassion about navigating students through the ups and downs of their faith. This is a must read for everyone working with teens — youth workers, parents and pastors. I highly recommend this book to you."

– REV. GREG SPECK, youth and family communicator for
youth leadership

"Written with refreshing honesty, great vulnerability, and trademark humor, Dugan Sherbondy breathes hope into anybody who has ever wondered: *God, where are you? I'm so excited for students, student ministry leaders, and parents to get their hands on this!"

– MIKE BREAUX, author and teaching pastor at
Heartland Community Church

PRAISE FOR **NEVER ALONE**

"It's obvious that Dugan is a gifted speaker who will impact the lives of students he meets. But the honesty and humor in *Never Alone* show that whether we're thirteen or sixty-three, we can all relate with feeling like God abandons us from time to time. I definitely recommend *Never Alone* if you want to hear the clearly communicated truth that in reality God never leaves us, nor forsakes us."

– KEITH ELGIN, recording artist and worship pastor at Vine Church

"Dugan Sherbondy is an important voice to the next generation. This book will be part of shaping and molding students into Godly men and women. It's fun to read, but also packed full of important content for people of any age. Every student and leader will benefit and grow from reading this book."

– ANNIE F. DOWNS, author of *Let's All Be Brave*

Editing by Steven Yaccino
Copy Editing by Joy Neal
Book design by LindsayLetters

First Printing, 2015

ISBN 978-0-9961965-0-5

Dugan Sherbondy
www.NeverAloneTheBook.com
www.DuganSherbondy.com
DuganESherbondy@gmail.com

NEVER ALONE

FOLLOWING GOD
WHEN YOU CAN'T FEEL HIM

DUGAN SHERBONDY

CONTENTS

CONTENTS

This book is dedicated to Vickie Norris, a friend and mentor during my high school and college years. She is also the reason this book was written.

Vickie, you were a wonderful mentor during a time when God was growing me in a lot of uncomfortable ways. Your wisdom, patience, love, and gentle correction was used by God to impact me far beyond what I'm sure you're aware of. In particular, your sense of God's Spirit prompting you to talk to me during the One Thing conference has forever marked me as being one of the most encouraging moments of my life at a time when I was desperate for understanding.

Know that God is continuing to use your influence to encourage others who find themselves unable to feel God. My prayer is that this book brings the same hope and encouragement to others that you once gave me.

Love,
Dugan

FORWARD

Thirteen years ago, shortly after we started our band *BarlowGirl,* we were unexpectedly approached by a record label. It wasn't just any record label, it was our dream record label, and next thing we knew they were offering us a developmental deal to make an album.

Never before had we felt so clearly that God had bigger plans for us and our music. For months, we poured every ounce of our energy into that project. We dropped out of school. We quit our jobs.

Then without warning, it was all over. In a matter of days and through a number of events, we found ourselves label-less, school-less and job-less. And on top of it all, as if we weren't panicking enough, suddenly we couldn't hear God anymore. Not even a whisper.

For hours, we would pray together, but in our time of need,

it was like He had simply abandoned us. We were scared and confused and wondering if we had maybe missed God all together. It was hard to have hope and hard to keep pressing in, but we were desperate. When we felt like we just couldn't pray anymore, we decided maybe we should write about what we were going through.

We sat down with a guitar and opened our journals and out poured the words: *I waited for you today, but you didn't show.*

It was then we had our "aha!" moment. It was in that moment we remembered that in His word, God promises us that He would never leave us or forsake us (Deuteronomy 31:6). And we had to remind ourselves that feelings don't set us free, but God's word always does. We had to remind ourselves that no matter what we were feeling, even if we couldn't feel or hear it, He was there. He promised He would be, and He is faithful to His promises.

The lyrics continued to flow from our hearts: *I cried out with no reply and I can't feel you by my side so I'll hold tight to what I know, you're here, and I'm never alone.*

Writing that song was a turning point for us, and we have never been the same since. It's why we love this book. Because admit it or not, a lot of us have gone through that season of God's silence. It's not something that should be ignored. Rather, it's something God can use to change your life and relationship with Him forever.

We have been friends with Dugan since we were young, and we love the story that he is telling. Much of what you'll read about in this book is the journey that he shared with us while we were going through our similar journey, which helped inspire the song we wrote in this season called "Never Alone."

Our hope is that this book will help you on your own journey of discovering God more. More than anything, may it help you navigate the times when you most doubt that God is nearby. May it help you know, without a doubt, that with God, you really are never alone.

Lauren, Alyssa, and Rebecca Barlow

NEVER ALONE

BARLOWGIRL

I waited for you today
But you didn't show
No no no
I needed You today
So where did You go?

You told me to call
Said You'd be there
And though I haven't seen You
Are You still there?

We cannot separate
'Cause You're part of me
And though You're invisible
I'll trust the unseen

And though I cannot see You
And I can't explain why
Such a deep, deep reassurance
You've placed in my life

I cried out with no reply
And I can't feel You by my side
So I'll hold tight to what I know
You're here and I'm never alone

CHAPTER ONE

WHEN GOD LEFT ME

The first time I saw Redwood National Park, I left with a full-body rash and a new rule against peeing near poison ivy.

It was 2002, and the trip started the way any good high school road trip should start: loading a conversion van at midnight with camping gear, Mountain Dew, and enough beef jerky to feed the International Space Station for a few months.

It ended the way no road trip of any kind should ever end: driving through Death Valley at midnight with poison ivy, which felt like an open oven on my red, oozing, irritated skin. It was gross. And uncomfortable. So gross and uncomfortable, in fact, that I ended up flying home early from Las Vegas and missed the rest of the trip. I was pretty bummed. Pretty itchy and pretty bummed.

It had otherwise been one of those unforgettable, Hollywood-montage-worthy vacations. Picture five teenage boys driving across the country in a vehicle that can only be described as the offspring of a shipping crate and a morbidly obese minivan. Without the modern convenience of Internet radio, we were forced to change the station ever hour or so as we traveled in and out of range, inevitably finding a new signal just in time to hear a new D.J. from Middle Of, Iowa, or Nowhere, Wyoming, talk over the intro to my favorite song.

I remember playing Frisbee with strangers at gas stations. I remember sitting around the campfire and talking about God and sin and girls and our future. We laughed a lot, cried a little, and even prayed for each other as the fire died out and the stars became brighter above us.

Me and the guys (I'm second from the right)

I remember sleeping in a tent next to the crystal blue waters of Lake Tahoe, surrounded by lush, green mountains. I remember the sun was shining and the air was crisp as we raced down the one-hundred-foot pier in the early morning and plunged into the water, knowing it would be icy but not caring. It was so picturesque—like swimming in a postcard.

But the highlight of that trip, despite the poison ivy, was visiting the redwood forest in Northern California. Being there is like visiting another planet—130,000 acres filled with some of the most incredible beauty on earth. Trees tower above you. Mist crawls through the underbrush. There is a calm, deafening silence there. The kind that makes you hold your breath for fear of ruing the moment.

Not only are they stunningly beautiful, but the redwoods are also fascinating trees. For example, they've been around since the time of the dinosaurs and once covered millions of miles of our planet. Their bark is fire proof and can be more than a foot thick. They are poisonous to tree pests and resistant to water rot. They're even resistant to battery acid, though this is perhaps only useful if you're ever fighting aliens with Sigourney Weaver.

They're so big, they seem fake. One redwood contains enough lumber to build forty modest-sized homes. They're longer than three blue whales or ten school buses, and if a single tree was made into wood planks that were laid end to end, it would stretch over a hundred miles—roughly a fourth the length of the state of Florida! They're so big, each tree requires hundreds of gallons of water a day to stay alive. Hundreds!

Today, we can walk among trees that were alive at the same time Jesus walked the earth. And for that reason alone, standing at the foot of a redwood is humbling. Not in a way that makes you feel insignificant, like outer space or the Grand Canyon. It's humbling in a way that makes you realize that a three-hundred-foot natural skyscraper was once shorter than a redheaded high schooler with poison ivy. It's humbling because it's enormous...and still growing.

One reason that redwoods are so massive and majestic is their root system. They are not like normal trees, which look like mirror images of themselves underground, with an individual root system that goes just about as deep and wide as the tree above. Redwood roots, on the other hand, only go about five or ten feet deep but spread out hundreds of feet in all directions, intertwining and fusing with other roots around them, creating a sturdy foundation for each individual tree and the forest itself.

. . . .

Growing up, I often felt like a redwood connected to many other root systems. When it came to my faith in God, I didn't have to work very hard to grow; it just happened naturally within my surroundings. My faith was situational. I didn't have to search for any kind of "spiritual water" because it was all around me.

I'm one of those people who usually says, "I've been a Christian my whole life." I grew up in a Christian household with Christian parents. I had Christian friends, read Christian books, watched Christian movies, and listened to Christian music - or at least the few good ones we had in the 1990s, like Five Iron Frenzy, Grammatrain, and DC Talk (honorable mentions to MxPx, Switchfoot, and Pedro the Lion).

My family would go to church services twice a week, where I also volunteered in the children's ministry. I was taught to read my Bible, pray, tithe, and take communion. And I was homeschooled, which meant I even did Christian school curriculum. (By the way, not all homeschooled kids live in their basement and make their own clothes out of wheat. Most of us are pretty normal. We just have the option to do algebra in our pajamas.)

I saw and felt God's presence through things like singing worship songs or the love I received from my friends. I grew to know Him through reading the Bible, prayer, and hearing teachings about Him. I had an increasing desire to honor God more with my decisions and avoid disobeying Him as best I could.

Things were good. God was good. Life was good. Everything seemed to be clicking. I mean, it wasn't perfect and there were tough things like breakups and sin struggles and seasons of pain. But overall, life following God felt solid, like it was going to be a firm foundation for the rest of my life.

Until God left me.

Until I couldn't feel or sense Him anymore.

It was as if, at some point without me noticing, He slipped out of the room. And now He was just... gone.

The foundation that my entire life was built on was suddenly and completely yanked out from under me.

I was a high school student already considering a career as a pastor, and I found myself getting the silent treatment from the Creator of the universe and the God I'd been following for most of my life.

I grew up surrounded by God, people of God, a church devoted to God, even math problems that mentioned God, but suddenly He just packed His bags and said "peace out!"

I felt totally alone. And as it continued, my faith, a faith I'd had for most of my life, slowly started to erode.

I was hurt.

And confused.

And lonely.

And angry.

And bitter.

And afraid.

And I didn't know what to do.

It was like a close relative or friend had just died, and I was left all alone to try and figure out how to deal with it.

As this continued, I went through all the stages of grief, plus like thirty more stages that I didn't even know existed.

First was denial. I would tell myself, *I can still totally feel Him, just not as strong...* So I'd fake it by raising my hands at church as if I felt something. Or I'd pray out loud with passion even though I had none. I'd talk to my youth pastor about a powerful, emotional moment during a church service even though it felt a million miles away. Then I'd get home and journal the exact opposite. *God, where were you tonight?*

Then I just got angry. I mean, come on! I'd literally devoted the majority of my life to God. I went to church, prayed, even volunteered. Now He's just going to vanish? Who does that?

I'm sure a lot of it was self-pity. Poor little Christian Dugan, who did almost everything right, was being treated unfairly. But my bitterness was real. This was totally His fault. All I felt like doing was walking out of church for the last time, looking up at the sky and firmly saying, "Screw you, God...if you're even there!"

I tried bargaining with God: *If I prayed for this person or that person or read this many Bible verses each day, then will You come back?*

Insecurity set in: *Was He mad? Was it something I did? Something I didn't do?*

And doubt took hold: *Was He never there in the first place? Had I been duped?*

Then I felt lonely. I'd grown up doing life with God, and now he was gone. I think this was the worst pain, because being or even just feeling alone goes against the very way we were created to live. Nothing can cause us more pain or fear than being alone.

Then the Lord God said, "It is not good for the man to be alone." – Genesis 2:18

God made us for relationship with Himself and with other people. We weren't meant to live life alone. There's something wrong with loneliness and we sense it in our core. That's what I felt.

It didn't get any better from there. It was like I had just gone through a breakup and was watching happy couples holding hands around every corner. Or like I was on a diet and all my friends wanted to go to Five Guys for lunch. Or like my dog had just died and I was watching a commercial with Sarah McLachlan singing about rescuing sad puppies. Or like I had a dairy allergy and was standing around at a free milkshake party. (All true stories, by the way, except for the milkshake party, which sounds like a great idea.)

I would be in a church service among hundreds of people who were clearly feeling, sensing, or experiencing God. They would be raising their hands in worship or quietly praying on their knees. I would watch this and grow more and more confused and angry. Apparently I was the only person God decided to ditch for no reason.

I started to resent my small group. I became bored with the Bible. It was the first time in my life that I wondered if Christianity was even worth my time.

Then I hit the final two stages of grief: depression and acceptance. These two stages blurred together for me. Over the course of a few years, I slipped into something that I can only describe as a spiritual funk. It was a depression that affected every other part of me. Spiritually, physically, and emotionally, I began to disconnect. I wanted nothing to do with God or anything having to do with Him. I accepted that God left me and gave up on figuring out how to get Him back.

All because I couldn't *feel* Him. God walked away from me, why shouldn't I walk away from Him?

I felt like a giant redwood that was suddenly and completely without water. My foundation was gone, my whole reality uprooted. And without this water I'd gotten so used to, my spiritual life began to wither away.

That's what it feels like when God leaves you.

CHAPTER TWO

EMOTIONS

When you can't feel God anymore, suddenly the most powerful spiritual experiences of your past become suspicious.

Statistics today show that between 65 and 85 percent of students will walk away from their faith after high school—and 23 percent of them do so within their first three years of college.

I was almost one of them. And not for the reasons you might think, but in part due to a reason that few student ministries have in the forefront of their minds: *emotional expectations.*

Like so many other teenage Christians, a major part of the reason I almost walked away from my faith was because it was founded on unrealistic expectations of what it felt like to follow God.

My faith was built on an emotion-based Christianity. One that was unsustainable. Once that emotion left, I questioned whether it was ever real in the first place.

Years later, I am a youth pastor. It is my job to teach junior high, high school, and college students about what it means to follow Jesus. My job is to help spark an authentic desire in them to grow closer to God. But if I'm going to be honest, it's not always rewarding work.

I've learned that student ministry (while super fun) can often times be a fruitless ministry. A more optimistic description is that it is a *seed-planting* ministry. And for any of you who have ever gardened, you know that growth takes time. You don't get to harvest right away.

It takes time for seeds of faith to grow. And as students graduate and move away, there are times that I don't get to see their lives transform as they grow into mature Christian adults. And that's hard.

With the best intentions, like my former youth pastors from long ago, I've longed for some sign that God is doing *something* in students' lives—especially in a way that affirms the time and energy I've poured into them. Sometimes you need a reminder that you're making a difference.

And in those times, it doesn't get any better than "Cry Night."

"Cry Night" is exactly what it sounds like. During a retreat, there is always one evening when students' emotions are most primed. It's the night when students surrender their past, admit their sins, cross the line of faith, raise their hands in worship, hug each other, stand arm-in-arm while swaying to worship songs, and yes, cry.

It's all very emotional.

The stories from small group leaders the next morning usually start with "There wasn't a dry eye…" or "All my guys wept as they prayed for Austin…" or "My girls kept saying they hadn't sobbed like that long in a while."

Score one for the youth pastor!

Student ministries use terms like "spiritual high" or "camp high" to talk about these life-changing moments in a student's relationship with God. As snot runs down teenagers' faces, student ministry leaders encourage them to remember how real the feeling of God is in that moment and not go back to regular life as if nothing had changed.

It's presented as the students' responsibility to cling to that emotional experience.

I believe these kinds of nights can be powerful, true and authentic. Any time you get to watch God move and watch students encounter God at a new level, it should be celebrated!

However, I've come to believe that too many youth groups are exploiting the emotional state of teenage students—in part because of very good intentions and in part to feel some sense of vocational accomplishment.

If my personal experiences are any barometer, I strongly believe things like "Cry Night" and the emotion-based Christianity they represent can contribute to the reasons many students consider walking away from their faith as they get older.

It was for me.

My early Christian life was chock full of emotionally charged moments with God. I remember which favorite worship songs would always evoke tears and passionate hand raising. I remember the powerful and emotional communion message the last night of our church summer camp that caused me to re-surrender my life to Christ (for the 3rd time in as many years) as I wept at the foot of a wooden cross on the stage. I remember standing with my small group, each of us with our arms around each other as we swayed together during a worship night. I remember feeling a rush of emotion and my heart rate increase as I felt God's presence surround me.

It was real. It was true. But the danger came when I started to associate what I was feeling with whether or not God was present and moving. This set me up for a long, hard fall once I didn't feel that feeling any more.

Students all around the nation experience Christianity this same way. Too often, I fear, young believers are taught to expect an emotional interaction with God and start looking for the emotion, versus looking for God. Or they simply aren't properly educated on the reality of emotions in moments with God.

This can happen in really extreme cases, as seen in the documentary *Jesus Camp*, which depicts students being pressured into having emotional experiences (or at least *acting* like they are having intense emotional experiences). Or in more mild cases, like "Cry Nights" and weekly worship services. Both are well-intentioned, yet both generally tend to target a student's emotions in order to elicit a response. This can be particularly dangerous when combined with the way pop-culture models emotion for young people throughout their everyday life.

In turn, student ministries are at risk of breeding a generation addicted to emotion. Many students are chasing after their next fix, not necessarily the One whose movement in their lives causes them to feel that spiritual sensation in the first place. *Emotion* becomes their god. Are students becoming emotional junkies, instead of disciples who seek after God?

A couple years ago, my friend Randi was leading an eighth grade girls small group at a middle school retreat. Most of the girls had been on a handful of retreats before and knew all about "Cry Night" (although they didn't know we called it that). During their Saturday night small group, Randi's girls were frustrated and feeling guilty that they hadn't cried during the message that night. They were frustrated that the teaching wasn't about surrender. Randi replied, "But you guys know this stuff! You know how to surrender and connect with God. Why do you need to cry to make that real?"

With so much focus on feeling an emotional response to God moving in their lives, they completely missed God! **They were hoping to feel something, but they actually missed everything.**

And if we're going to be honest, it's not entirely their fault.

Youth leaders bear some responsibility for this, particularly because students are at a developmental state that makes them, to put it bluntly, emotional gluttons. Intentional or not, most student ministries feed those cravings by creating experiences with the wonderful intentions of connecting students to God, but those experiences often times end up focusing too much on connecting students with the emotion of God instead.

A student's emotional response is payday for student pastors because it's a tangible sign of God moving in their ministry. But are we giving an appropriate amount of consideration to the long-term effect that emotion-based Christianity has on students and their spiritual health? I'm as guilty of this as anyone. A few years ago, I was teaching at a retreat for a middle school ministry I was leading. A year before, halfway through the closing worship set on Saturday night, there wasn't a dry eye in the house. But during that second retreat, something was different and I began to doubt myself.

Everything was pretty much the same: passionate teaching about God's love, dynamic worship music, devoted leaders engaging with their students, etc. The only thing different was that on Saturday night, the tissue boxes remained full. Nobody cried.

Did I do something wrong?

Did I not do something I should have?

Was my teaching not good enough?

Should we have changed that one worship song?

Did I fail the students somehow?

I found myself striving for another emotional response from students to assure me that everything was OK, that I was good at my job, that God was moving.

I don't think I was aware of what I was doing, but the truth is that, in certain ways, I was exploiting the emotions of the students that I loved. At best, I was expecting too much from them emotionally. At worst, I was subconsciously manipulating them. And I think there are count-less student ministries around the country doing the same thing.

Students, in turn, need to understand the pure biology of their brains, so that when a time comes that they start to feel God differently—perhaps less potently—they don't abandon their faith entirely.

. . . .

Students, there is a full-steam feelings factory in your brain.

Every emotion you feel—joy, stress, fear, anger, love—is the result of chemicals released by your limbic system in the lower rear part of the brain and then absorbed by your neurons. Depending on what you're seeing, thinking or experiencing, chemicals like dopamine and serotonin are quite literally invading your mind and causing you to feel. (Bet you weren't expecting to get an awesome science lesson were you?!)

You cannot escape these "emotional chemicals" any more than you can drink Red Bull and not feel energized or take Tylenol PM and not feel sleepy. The brain releases these chemicals that our system absorbs and then we "feel."

Unlike the front part of your brain, which processes thought and logic, experts refer to the emotional part of the brain as the "lower" or "inferior" part. Sure takes the magic out of a movie like *The Notebook*, huh? Although I'm sure Ryan Gosling's limbic system looks pretty good with it's shirt off.

the human **BRAIN**

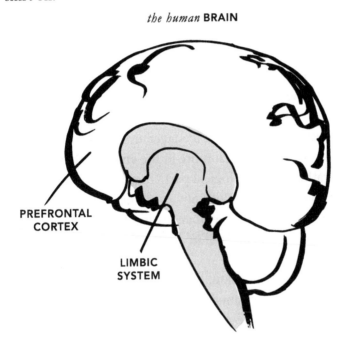

These two parts of the brain are constantly in relationship with each other. The prefrontal cortex is essentially in charge of managing the emotional chemicals released by the limbic system. Whenever a chemical is released because of outside stimuli, the logical part of the brain takes over to process that emotion to determine its legitimacy.

And biologically speaking, the teenage brain is under emotional siege.

In an interview titled "Inside the Teenage Brain," produced by PBS' *Frontline*, Deborah Yurgelun-Todd, professor of psychiatry and director of the Cognitive Neuroimaging Laboratory at the University of Utah, concluded from her study that the brains of teenagers actually respond differently than the brains of adults when processing external information that evokes an emotional response. Actually, they respond *very* differently, with the most dramatic difference being in the earlier teen years.

According to her studies, a teenager, unlike an adult, processes information much more in the emotional part of the brain, rather than the logical part. There is nothing good or bad about it, but biologically speaking, a teenager feels emotion in a stronger way than an adult would because parts of their brain are still in development.

In a fully developed brain, first the limbic system releases a chemical based on outside circumstances that make a person feel. Then, the prefrontal cortex kicks in to logically process that emotion and why it was felt. But a teenager's prefrontal cortex is pretty much dormant during this process. Meaning they experience the full strength of their emotions without the mental ability to logically process them through the filters that an adult mind would.

"The teenage brain is a work in progress," wrote Sandra Witelson, a neuroscientist at McMaster University in Ontario. And in a 2005 article for *U.S. News & World Report*, journalist Shannon Brownlee is quoted with describing the teenage limbic system as "entering a stage of development in which it goes into hyperdrive."

As time goes on, the relationship between the front part and lower part of the brain develops and becomes more balanced, but it's believed that our brains aren't fully developed until our early-to-mid-twenties.

This has huge implications for the way students experience a relationship with God.

Because of the amazing grace of God, life-changing commitments to Christ often come in a moment of intense and emotional self-realization, when we admit how messed up we are and embrace our vulnerabilities. More often than not, when students tell me about the moment they decided to surrender their life to Christ, it is depicted in emotional terms. It was during an altar call at a retreat or during a powerful teaching on God's love or Jesus' death. Many times students use phrases like, "I just felt totally broken..." or "It felt like God was wrapping His arms around me..." or "For the first time, I felt like this weight had been lifted off my shoulders."

And I don't doubt them for a second. I have felt God's presence that powerfully. He was, after all, the One who created us with the ability to feel and to experience these spiritual interactions.

I'm not saying emotions are bad because they're not!

They're awesome! I realize I might get some angry letters about this from my Vulcans readers (and there are *a lot* of them), but among the plethora of wisdom from Star Trek director J.J. Abrams, even Spock learned the power and joy of emotion as seen in Star Trek. It's awesome to feel love and chemistry towards someone. It's great to feel excitement at the top of a roller coaster or anticipation before opening night of your school play. It's okay to feel nervous before a test or angry at a friend who says something hurtful. It's okay to feel sad when a pet dies or that jolt of fear during *The Walking Dead.*

There's nothing wrong with emotions. Emotions are an important and vital part of what it means to be human.

I'm not campaigning for an emotionless Christianity. The Bible is filled with examples of the emotional responses people experienced when the power and presence of God showed up in their lives. David's emotion came out in songs; Moses felt fear when seeing God's back; the disciples felt passion and excitement throughout their journey following Jesus. Those that Jesus healed were described as having incredible joy, the woman who anointed Jesus' feet fell down at His feet in tears as the emotion of her gratitude overflowed, and the list goes on.

The problem *isn't* when we feel emotion. **The problem is when a young Christian enters a relationship with Jesus through an emotional experience and then continues to seek that same emotional experience as evidence that**

their faith is real.

Because of this, many don't know how to connect with God on a daily basis without some emotional sensation—or, for some, without the sense of brokenness and helplessness they felt when they first surrendered to Jesus.

I am thirty years old. I am a pastor. I can say with confidence that I may never experience God with the same emotion that I did when I was fourteen years old. Does that make me less of a Christian? Does that mean I never truly sensed God's presence in my life? Absolutely not! But when God went missing in action during my high school years, I did believe that.

Should we really be surprised that some young Christians go on to seek out worldly experiences that offer them the same kind of emotional high they once got from following Jesus?

Youth groups aren't the only arenas where students are appealed to on basis of emotion. We live in a culture constantly driven by emotions. We say things like, "It felt like the right thing to do in the moment..." or "What is your heart telling you?" We seek an emotional rush for the pure purpose of feeling something. Skydiving, bungee jumping, hang gliding, chick flicks, and binge-watching *Breaking Bad* are all meant to help us feel things like excitement, fear, adrenaline, or sadness (for Mr. White). Emotions are why the horror movie genre exists! Nobody *likes* scary movies. You see them to get that adrenaline rush of fear when there's a jump scene or that chill in your bones when you find out Bruce Willis is a ghost.

This reality can even lead to some very unhealthy habits and addictions, like drugs or alcohol or pornography—sometimes because we need something more intense to help us feel, and sometimes because we're looking for something that can numb what we don't want to feel.

We live in this world that says if it feels good, do it. And if it doesn't, then avoid it at all costs. **But the truth about emotions is that they are one of the weakest foundations to build our lives on.**

John Ortberg wrote in his book *Soul Keeper* (2014) about the danger of our external lives influencing our internal state. "I was operating on the unspoken assumption that my inner world would be filled with life, peace, and joy once my external world was perfect." He then writes, "That's a great recipe for a healthy soul, as long as you live in a perfect world."

But we don't live in a perfect world, as he goes on to point out. We don't live in a world that can offer us true happiness all the time. In fact we live in a broken world that's filled with pain and difficulty. Jesus even talks about this:

"Here on earth you will have many trials and sorrows.

But take heart, because I have overcome the world."
– John 16:33b

Jesus never said, "Hey, once you follow me, you're going
to feel good all the time!" If anything, He talked way more
about how following Him might actually lead to persecu-
tion and pain and difficulty.

In John 10:10, Jesus says, *"The thief's purpose is to steal
and kill and destroy. My purpose is to give them a rich and
satisfying life."*

I was taught that when Jesus said "thief," he was talking
about Satan. That made sense. I mean, yeah, the enemy
of God would try and hurt the people God loves most, by
stealing, killing, and destroying. But when you read this
verse in the context of what Jesus is talking about in John
10, he's actually not talking about the devil at all. When Jesus uses the term "thief," what he's actually referring to are
the things and people in the world that will try and convince us that they can offer us life—even though they can't.
Things like work, grades, boyfriends, girlfriends, success,
friends, possessions, money, and even false spirituality.
We think these things offer true happiness and that we can
truly experience life through them. But they are all tempo-
rary. Over and over again, they fall way short, leaving us
empty and wanting more.

And so we move on to the next thing. I almost did.

God was not meeting my emotional expectations, and I was done. I was ready to say, "Thanks for the memories!"

But then I had a conversation with someone that changed my thinking entirely.

CHAPTER THREE

EMMAUS

My life changed in Kansas City, on the road to Emmaus…
which actually isn't anywhere near Missouri.

Let me explain.

I was a junior in high school and, despite my spiritual
funk, I decided to go with a group of people from my
church to a Christian conference, not expecting much other than another road trip with beef jerky and a good time.

It was a conference on New Year's Eve that consisted of
twelve hours (you read that right) of worship beginning at
noon on December 31 and going until after midnight on
January 1 to usher in the year 2002.

The event was held in an enormous conference center with
a huge stage, loud music, bright lights, and thousands of

people all having an amazing experience of worship.

Except for me.

Thousands of people were there raising their hands, closing their eyes, shedding tears, on their knees, jumping, dancing, praying, hugging, cheering, yelling. And there I was, standing in the middle of it all with my hands in my pockets, angry and wondering why God was so clearly with everyone else but me. I remember wondering how many times I could make up an excuse to go the bathroom, just so I could leave for a few minutes without raising serious concerns over the health or size of my bladder.

Around six in the evening, after we'd been singing for about six hours, a woman named Vickie, who had been a teacher and mentor to me during this time, got my attention. She was sitting a few chairs to my left in the same aisle and leaned forward to catch my eye. She motioned for me to follow her. I shrugged and obliged, glad to escape the God fest that I felt so disconnected from.

She led me out of the room and into a huge cafeteria, where I slumped into a chair across the table from her. I wasn't looking forward to the conversation. I thought she was going to tell me to worship more or ask me something about God or why I wasn't singing much or what was wrong with me. Then I'd have to fake some excuse about being tired or that I was just silently praying or something to avoid talking about what was really bothering me.

But then she asked, "Dugan, do you feel God?"

I had to quickly choke back tears. It was the first time anybody had correctly identified and asked me about what was going on inside me. I looked down at the floor and fidgeted a little. For a split second I debated whether or not I should be honest. But I didn't have the strength to fake it anymore.

"No," I said quietly. "I haven't for a while."

"I thought so," she said, nodding.

She paused for a second, but it felt like an hour. Then she asked me to read a passage from the Bible. She turned to Luke 24 and slid the book across the table to me. "Start at verse thirteen," she said.

It was a passage that took place after Jesus had been crucified, but His disciples didn't know about the resurrection part yet. At that time, Jesus' closest friends and followers believed He had failed. They thought He was the promised Messiah, but they had watched Him be tortured. They believed He was the Son of God, but they had watched Him be humiliated. They believed He was the key to life and God's Kingdom, but they had watched Him die a criminal's death.

Confused, lost, maybe even angry or embarrassed, the disciples weren't sure what to do next or what was going to happen to them.

And in the midst of all that, two of Jesus' disciples were walking together on a road from Jerusalem to a town called Emmaus. Most likely, they were going to share the bad news about Jesus' death with people who hadn't heard about it yet.

I started reading:

Now that same day two of them were going to a village called Emmaus, about seven miles from Jerusalem. They were talking with each other about everything that had happened. As they talked and discussed these things with each other, Jesus himself came up and walked along with them; but they were kept from recognizing him.

He asked them, "What are you discussing together as you walk along?"

They stood still, their faces downcast. One of them, named Cleopas, asked him, "Are you only a visitor to Jerusalem and do not know the things that have happened there in these days?"

"What things?" he asked.

"About Jesus of Nazareth," they replied. "He was a prophet, powerful in word and deed before God and all the people. The chief priests and our rulers handed him over to be sentenced to death, and they crucified him; but we had hoped that he was the one who was going to redeem Israel. And

what is more, it is the third day since all this took place. In addition, some of our women amazed us. They went to the tomb early this morning but didn't find his body. They came and told us that they had seen a vision of angels, who said he was alive. Then some of our companions went to the tomb and found it just as the women had said, but him they did not see."

He said to them, "How foolish you are, and how slow to believe all that the prophets have spoken! Did not the Messiah have to suffer these things and then enter his glory?" And beginning with Moses and all the Prophets, he explained to them what was said in all the Scriptures concerning himself.

As they approached the village to which they were going, Jesus continued on as if he were going farther. But they urged him strongly, "Stay with us, for it is nearly evening; the day is almost over." So he went in to stay with them.

When he was at the table with them, he took bread, gave thanks, broke it and began to give it to them. Then their eyes were opened and they recognized him, and he disappeared from their sight. They asked each other, "Were not our hearts burning within us while he talked with us on the road and opened the Scriptures to us?"

They got up and returned at once to Jerusalem. There they found the Eleven and those with them, assembled together and saying, "It is true! The Lord has risen and has appeared to Simon." Then the two told what had happened on the way, and how Jesus was recognized by them when he broke the bread. – Luke 24:13-35

So these two guys thought Jesus had failed. They were defeated, discouraged, and afraid. Jesus shows up and starts walking with them, but then there are those seven crazy words: *But they were kept from recognizing him* (vs. 16).

Wait, who kept them from recognizing Jesus? *God* did!?!

Why would God hide Himself from anyone, let alone His own followers?

It was one of the most bizarre accounts from the Bible I'd ever read—a story about God literally walking with people who had no idea He was even there.

Vickie said, "*The first thing I want you to notice is that God was with them...even though they couldn't feel Him.*"

I kept staring at the open Bible in front of me. She was right. It was clear that God was with them. Even though they didn't know it, even though they didn't recognize Him, even though they couldn't feel Him, He was there. Right next to them! And these were guys who had followed Jesus in person! If anyone would have recognized Him, it would have been them!

It was the first time I'd ever heard that.

Was it possible that God was with me, and I just couldn't feel Him? Was it possible that this entire time I was pleading and pissed off and feeling desperately alone, He was right next to me and I just couldn't recognize it?

Was it possible that my emotions and perceptions weren't the best factor in determining God's presence?

After hearing about the disciples' bizarre walk to Emmaus, I still needed more proof.

I mean, maybe this was a one-time fluke in the Bible—the one and only time when God was present and people didn't know. The single anomaly in the Bible where He intentionally hid Himself from people. I needed some more convincing.

Well, as it turns out, the Bible is filled (FILLED!) with passages written by people who felt like God went AWOL on them.

In fact, throughout Scripture there are numerous examples that make clear the spiritual loneliness I was going through was not only common, but something each one of us should be prepared to face at one point or another in our lives. Each example makes clear that knowing and trusting in the truth (that God might at times be incognito, but not inattentive) is far more important than whether we immediately see or feel Him in the moment.

In Genesis 28, for instance, Jacob had a dream while sleeping in the middle of the desert. He fall asleep on a rock (somehow) and had a psychedelic dream about a stairway to heaven, with God up at the top saying in his best game-show-host voice, *"I am with you and will protect you wherever you go."*

When Jacob woke up, he said, *"Surely the Lord is in this place, and I was not aware of it."*

What a crazy, even scary thought. That God could be so close to us and we not even know it! I knew exactly how Jacob felt.

Another example comes a few books later. After the death of Moses (who was like the Israelite's version of the Pope or Billy Graham), God called Joshua to lead His people to the Promised Land. To sum it up, God said this to the new leader of the Israelites:

"Be strong and of good courage; do not be afraid, nor be dismayed, for the Lord your God is with you wherever you go." – Joshua 1:9

Pretty inspiring stuff, especially coming directly from God. But when you examine it closely, one question emerges: Why would God have to tell Joshua that He would always be with him if it was guaranteed that Joshua would sense and see and feel God constantly?

Because that's not what it was going to be like to follow God!

Joshua was going to experience fear and discouragement and confusion at times when he felt like God had deserted him. He would experience moments or seasons when he might not feel God or be able to sense His presence, just like us. And in those moments, Joshua would have to remember what God told him at the beginning of his whole journey: that he is not alone, and that God would be with him "wherever he went."

. . . .

Sitting in that Kansas City conference cafeteria, God was saying the same thing to me:

Dugan, there will be times when you will feel abandoned and discouraged. And in those times, you'll probably think I'm not there. But here's the truth: I am always with you. That's what I want you to believe in, more than what you see or feel.

Not convinced?

The Psalms are full of similar angsty spiritual-funk confessions:

O God, you are my God;
I earnestly search for you.

My soul thirsts for you;
   my whole body longs for you
in this parched and weary land
   where there is no water.
   – Psalm 63:1

For I am waiting for you, O Lord.
   You must answer for me, O Lord my God.
Do not abandon me, O Lord.
   Do not stand at a distance, my God.
   – Psalm 38:15; 21

Why do you look the other way?
   Why do you ignore our suffering and oppression?
   – Psalm 44:24

O Lord, why do you reject me?
   Why do you turn your face from me?
   – Psalm 88:14

O Lord, how long will you forget me? Forever?
   How long will you look the other way?

Turn and answer me, O Lord my God!
   – Psalm 13:1

These sure seem like the words of a person going through an emotionally difficult season, a time of not feeling God. They sound like the words of someone whose soul was totally dried out and dying of thirst for God. Or like he was waiting and waiting and waiting and waiting, feeling like God has abandoned him. I know a song by Dashboard Confessional or Taylor Swift can tap into your heart after a breakup, but these words from Psalms strike at some deep, core stuff when you can't feel God with you.

And consider that verse that you've undoubtedly seen in a frame hanging above your grandmother's toilet:

Your word is a lamp to my feet and a light to my path.
  – Psalm 119:105

Why would we need the Bible as a lamp and a light unless sometimes we're going to be walking in the dark! We might not see or feel God, but we have the Bible to help guide us in those times when His presence isn't felt.

Time after time, God's chosen people needed this reminder. Before Jesus walked the earth, the Israelites experienced four hundred years of silence from God. After speaking directly to His people, empowering prophets to speak for Him, and performing powerful miracles (the ten plagues of Egypt, parting of the Red Sea, leading Israel as a pillar of fire or smoke, and providing food and water, among others), God went mum. All the communication lines dried up. And it lasted for more than four centuries, during which people only heard stories of God speaking, but never experienced it for themselves.

Can you imagine how easy it would have been for them to

think God had up and left? But the truth is that God was prepping them for something better—the most powerful event in all of history.

He was preparing the world for His Son.

Even after Jesus arrived, there were plenty of times when people were unaware He was present. The morning that Jesus rose from the dead, Mary Magdalene went to the tomb to see for herself that it was empty. While she was there, she saw this guy who she thought was the gardener.

She turned to leave and saw someone standing there. It was Jesus, but she didn't recognize him. – John 20:14

Mary Magdalene, whom Jesus had saved from being stoned for adultery, who followed Jesus for years, who watched Him die. Even *she* didn't recognize Jesus!

Now for a big one: even Jesus Himself didn't always feel the presence of His Father.

Jesus, who was fully human and experienced all the things that we experience, knows what it's like to feel abandoned by God.

The night before He was killed, Jesus went to a garden to ask God, His Father, to save Him. There is no clearer example of a human wanting to be close to God than in that moment. It's God's own Son, crying out to Him for help.

"Abba, Father," he cried out, "everything is possible for you. Please take this cup of suffering away from me. Yet I want your will to be done, not mine." – Mark 14:35-36

You can see the desperation in His choice of words.

The word "Abba" was a term in the Aramaic language that was the commonly spoken language during that time. The term is most often translated as meaning "father," but the cultural context meant something much more personal and intimate. The best way to think of it in our modern-day language would be "daddy."

Jesus, in His most painful moment before the cross, reached out to His Father and essentially said, "Daddy...I need You." But God didn't descend on a chariot of fire and light. Instead, Jesus sat in a garden, seemingly alone, and by all indications, felt nothing.

And less than twenty-four hours later, the Bible makes it clear that God was indeed not with His Son as Jesus took His last breath, while hanging, beaten and bloody from a plank of wood.

The moment of Jesus' death, when he took the sin of mankind, God was not with Him. The whole reason Jesus came was to die the death we all deserved and conquer sin. God is holy and cannot be in the presence of sin, so Jesus had to take on sin so it would die with Him. That meant willingly experiencing something no one else on earth could come close to understanding: being separated from God. The best definition of that is hell.

Heaven is life with God and hell is complete separation from Him.

Jesus went through that.

Right before He died, Jesus called out to God, verbalizing the pain of not being with His Father for the first time ever.

At noon, darkness fell across the whole land until three o'clock. At about three o'clock, Jesus called out with a loud voice, "Eli, Eli, lema sabachthani?" which means "My God, my God, why have you abandoned me?"
– Matthew 27:45-46

This is a heartbreaking thing to picture. Not only was someone experiencing a complete lack of God's presence. But that person was God's own Son, and it was at the moment when He was most desperately lonely and craving God's presence.

And yet, God didn't show up.

Not because God didn't want to, not because God was mad or uncaring. The reason God didn't show up was because He loves you and me. He withdrew His presence and let His Son suffer and die so that Jesus could take on the sin of every human and then make a way for us to be with God.

. . . .

There are times when God intentionally hides from us, too. There are moments or seasons—sometimes really, really long ones—when God withholds the "feeling" of His presence. He did it with numerous people in the Bible, so it stands to reason that He would do it with us, as well.

But just because we can't feel God doesn't mean He isn't there. It's also not because we've done something wrong or because we aren't doing something right. It's simply because God is choosing to hide from us. He's choosing to withhold our ability to feel or recognize Him.

The Bible makes it clear that God's presence and love is not based on what we do or don't do.

In Romans 8:38-39, Paul writes:

And I am convinced that nothing can ever separate us from God's love. Neither death nor life, neither angels nor demons, neither our fears for today nor our worries about tomorrow—not even the powers of hell can separate us from God's love. No power in the sky above or in the earth below—indeed, nothing in all creation will ever be able to separate us from the love of God that is revealed in Christ Jesus our Lord.

Nothing can separate us from God and His love. I'll talk in the next chapter about why God chooses to hide Himself, but don't think for a second that it is because of something bad you've done. God's presence isn't based on our actions or evidenced by our emotions.

Regardless of the emotions you've experienced or lies you've believed, the truth is what can set you free.

That truth: you are never alone.

CHAPTER FOUR

HIDING

I have a three-year-old daughter named Eva (pronounced Ā-vuh), and in addition to an intense addiction to the color pink, she has an endless appetite for games. Most weeks I get to spend two or three full days hanging out with her from dawn until dusk. Those are my favorite days.

Aside the the occasional tantrum Eva throws when I try explaining why we can't go to Neverland on Saturday, or my hour-long effort to clean pink Play Dough out of the carpet (the trick is to replace the carpet), my weeks are mostly filled with sprinkling imaginary pixie dust and pretending to be a princess. I'm perfecting my ballerina twirl, which is coming along nicely (the trick is to wear a bright tutu, which distracts from my terrible technique).

The meaning behind a person's name has always been important to me, especially when thinking of my kids.

Eva's name means "life" and it was a name I'd always loved. It was partly inspired by listening to the music and hearing the story of Eva Cassidy, an incredible singer from Maryland who wasn't discovered until after she died of cancer at the age of thirty-three. So when my wife, Lindsay, and I found out we were having a girl, we decided to name her Eva Love. A girl full of life and love. And almost every night since she was born, we've prayed that God would fill her with life and love and help her bring life and love to other people.

And boy does she ever! She is so full of life! She loves to laugh and run, she loves to sing and have dance parties, and she loves to include everybody in a tri-state area in whatever activity she's doing at the moment. So if you're in a mall and hear a child yell, "Come on everybody! Let's twirl together!" It's probably Eva (true story), and please do join in.

One of Eva's favorite games is hide and seek—we play it all the time. Linds and I take turns hiding with her in the house while the other one counts to ten.

Eva is giddy when she jumps into my arms so we can hurry and find a spot to hide. Her little legs kick with joy and her smile takes over her face as we race through the house while Lindsay's "five…six…seven…" grows fainter. Soon we find a hiding spot that can fit us both. The best places so far include the shower, the closet, or the car. We squeeze in and I hold her close as we shut the door or close the curtain. As we stand in the darkness, she talks in the most adorable whisper while we wait to be found.

"Shhh…be quiet…" she says. "Mama's comin'..!"

"Ok!" I whisper back.

That's my favorite part. There is something profoundly special about watching my child understand this simple game with such intensity and joy. Even though we worked hard to find a great hiding spot, Eva's delight comes from knowing that no matter how hard she tries, she will never win this game. She will always be found.

Because she doesn't want to win. She wants to be found. I mean, hiding without being found is just called "Sitting Alone in the Closet." And according to my friends, that's a weird thing to do on Friday nights.

Without a doubt, Eva's favorite part of this game is the moment that her mama or I throw open the door or whip off the blanket or turn on the light to reveal her. "Found you!" we yell, as she laughs and squeals. We laugh and tickle her and she smiles and shakes with joy. Then without fail, she says, "AGAIN!" and we do it all over.

If Eva had it her way, this would go on for a few years or a few thousand games, whichever comes first.

When you stop and think about it, it's not too different

than the game we play with God early in our Christian lives. All of us, at one point or another, are found by God; and at some point, most of us become prodigal sons (or his equally messed up brother). We stray, he pursues, and we love being lost and found again. God enjoys it and we enjoy it, because there is equal joy in both finding and being found.

A thought recently struck me: When will I start hiding from Eva? When will she want to start finding me? Am I depriving her of half of the fun by always seeking her? I mean, sure I've "hidden" from her on occasion, but it's usually a very obvious place so she won't have to do much seeking. Under a blanket while snoring loudly, behind the couch with my head sticking out, in the pantry while singing every song from *Frozen*.

But as she grows up, our games are sure to become more challenging. Someday, she'll want me to hide from her for real. She won't immediately know where I'm at, which will require her to do some true seeking before she finds me. There might be a brief moment or two where she wonders if I've left. But that will only last until the moment she finds me.

In the same way, what if God likes being found just as much as I do? What if He doesn't want me to miss out on the seeking?

Especially because hide and seek is a game God is already

familiar with. In the Old Testament, some people who were assembling potential kings for Israel couldn't find Saul, so they asked God.

And the Lord replied, "He is hiding among the baggage." So they found him and brought him out, and he stood head and shoulders above anyone else. – 1 Samuel 10:22-23

Boom. Point God.

And this wasn't God's first point. He earned that back in Genesis when Adam and Eve hid from Him and He pretended not to know where they were.

When the cool evening breezes were blowing, the man and his wife heard the Lord God walking about in the garden. So they hid from the Lord God among the trees. Then the Lord God called to the man, "Where are you?" – Genesis 3:8-9

God *invented* hide and seek!

And He plays it.

But far too often, all we do is hide and expect to be found. Maybe there are times when it's our turn to find. What if you and God are both sitting in separate hiding spots waiting for the other to fling the door open, pull of the covers, flip on the light? After years of Him seeking you, is it your turn to count to ten?

Because God wants to be found.

God wants to be pursued.

But in order to be found, first He has to be hidden.

············

During my season of not feeling God, one significant encouragement I received was a book by a guy named Graham Cooke (who's British, so you know he's cool) called *Hiddenness and Manifestation.*

His main point, and the thing that most spoke to me, is the idea that we will all experience seasons when God's presence is "hidden" (where we can't feel Him) and seasons when God's presence is "manifested" (when we can feel Him). In both scenarios God is with us, the difference is simply whether we can feel His presence or not.

Cooke defines them both like this:

MANIFESTATION: The times when you feel God's presence and His touch upon your life in a very immediate way. He is just there! Those times are wonderful and effortless.

HIDDENNESS: Those times when you have to *believe* that you have peace with God, because you don't feel it in your emotions.

The idea of God being intentionally hidden was something I'd never heard of before, but something that I slowly began to get excited about as I came to understand and practice what it means to seek Him.

Because God promises that when we seek Him, we *will* find Him.

There's a famous Bible verse that comes from the book of Jeremiah, named after a prophet, in which God says the Israelites are going to be conquered and taken captive by the nation of Babylon. In case you're not sure, this is a bummer of a prophecy. To be told that you're about to be conquered and hauled off as slaves while your hometown is taken over by strangers would definitely fall into the category of "bad news."

Here's what God said:

"When seventy years are completed for Babylon, I will come to you and fulfill my good promise to bring you back to this place. For I know the plans I have for you," declares the Lord, "plans to prosper you and not to harm you, plans to give you hope and a future. Then you will call on me and come and pray to me, and I will listen to you. You will seek me and find me when you seek me with all your heart. I will be found by you," declares the Lord, "and will bring you back from captivity. I will gather you from all the nations and places where I have banished you," declares the Lord, "and will bring you back to the place from which I carried

you into exile." – Jeremiah 29:10-14 (NIV)

There are two key parts of this passage I want to point out.

The first one is verse 11: *"For I know the plans I have for you,"* declares the Lord, *"plans to prosper you and not to harm you, plans to give you hope and a future."* This is the famous verse that you're probably familiar with, and for good reason. It's an awesome verse. It's super encouraging to know that God created each of us for a purpose, that He has plans for us, and that we can rest in the hope that God has a future planned for us that will bless us with good.

What's interesting to note, however, is that God says this to his people right after telling them that an awful thing is going to happen.

God didn't say, "For I know the plans I have for you. They are plans for good and not for disaster, to give you a future with no more pain or difficulty or struggle or bad realty television on Bravo. It's all smooth sailing from here on out, as long as you stick with me!"

It wasn't like that at all.

Right when things were about to get a lot worse, God chose to tell His people that He has a future of blessings for them.

At first this seems kind of backwards. The immediate

future looked like the opposite of what God was saying. I wouldn't blame any Israelites who felt like God had deserted them and actually didn't care what happened to them at all.

But it makes sense. We don't need encouragement when things are going well. Instead, God tells his people life is going to get hard, but then he reminds them to hold on to His promise *despite* the difficulty coming. He reminds them that in the face of their circumstances, He is still in control.

Then in verse 12-14a God says, *"Then you will call on me and come and pray to me, and I will listen to you. You will seek me and find me when you seek me with all your heart. I will be found by you," declares the Lord…"*

Why would God have to remind His people that He is listening or that they will find Him? Maybe because it won't be clear to people that their prayers are being heard. He doesn't say that they will *see* Him or *feel* Him or *notice* an immediate response; He just makes it clear that He will hear them when they pray. That even as they pray, they might not have a sure sense that God is hearing them. In fact, they might strongly doubt it. But in those moments, God wants them to be reassured that He is there and He is listening.

Now what about your life? Do you think God has changed, or do you think the same is true for us? Whether or not we have a sense that God is listening, can we be confident He is there? Can we be confident that God has good plans for us, and that anything He does—including hiding His presence from us—is for our ultimate good?

CHAPTER FIVE

WHY

At this point, you might be asking *why?*

If God promises to never leave us, why intentionally hide Himself? At best, it's confusing. At worst, it's cruel. So why would He do it?

Sitting at the cafeteria table in Kansas City, I asked the same question.

Vickie told me God was with me, even though I couldn't feel Him. She told me He'd always been with me. She said that was the truth. And I wanted to believe her.

But in the back of my mind, this thought tugged at me until I couldn't ignore it. Why? I was beginning to understand *what* was going on, but shifting out of my spiritual funk depended on an explanation of *why* it was going on.

So I asked her.

"Vickie, why would God not let me feel Him if He's always with me?"

Without skipping a beat, she said, "Because He wants to speak to you, Dugan."

Um...what? If God wanted to speak to me, why would He prevent me from sensing Him? Isn't that counter-productive?

Let's look again at the road to Emmaus. When you read the rest of that passage, as Vickie and I did, Jesus did this interesting thing as He walked and talked with His disciples.

And beginning with Moses and all the Prophets, he explained to them what was said in all the Scriptures concerning himself. – Luke 24:27

During this period when the disciples did not recognize Jesus, He was teaching them about the Bible and Himself. He taught them all about the prophecies and promises He fulfilled. He taught them about the Messiah, the very man they were walking beside.

Remember, Jesus had just died and no one knew about His resurrection yet. If Jesus had told them it was Him, the disciples would have been way too distracted to listen to anything He had to say.

Amid the shock and elation, imagine how laughable it would have been for Jesus to try and stop His disciples from flipping out so He could walk them through some Old Testament theology.

If I was there, I would have said, "What? Who cares? I have to go tell all my friends! This is ten times more awesome than anything David Blaine has done! Plus way less creepy!"

Think about it. How many times did Jesus tell the disciples something that seems obvious to us when we read it now? He said over and over that He was going to die and then rise on the third day, but they totally missed it!

Why? Because they were watching this guy raise people from the dead! They watched Him heal people with life-long diseases, and multiply food to feed thousands of people, and walk on water. That's why!

They were so distracted by the incredible presence of Jesus that they would frequently miss the words of Jesus.

And so do we.

When we can feel Him, it's easy to get distracted by how amazing and wonderful God is and miss what He's saying to us.

When God's presence is manifested, we see Him, feel Him,

experience Him, feel His love, feel our love for Him, sense His power. We are on fire for Him, can't get enough of Him, love worshipping Him, love telling people about Him. Because the presence of God is both powerful and addicting!

But when God's presence is hidden, that's when our ears are most ready to listen. Like a blind person's other senses becoming enhanced because of their lack of vision, when our emotional sensations die down, our hearing perks up. Because it's all we have. Kind of like my new favorite super-hero, Daredevil, but with less punching.

Don't get me wrong—walking by faith can be difficult. *Really difficult.* It's like getting up in the middle of the night to get a drink of water when it is pitch black in the house. You have to slowly shuffle your feet a few inches at a time with your arms outstretched, hoping you won't blast your shin on the coffee table until you can get to a light switch. It's stressful and exhausting.

So is walking by faith. It takes effort to believe in the truth instead of what we feel or see right in front of us. It is a daily, moment-by-moment decision to believe in something bigger than what we feel. Something deeper and more significant: God's promise.

Maybe you do not feel God. Maybe you haven't felt Him for a long time. During worship or just in your spirit, you feel lonely and far away from God. And it has caused you to distance yourself from Him and the people around you. It's caused you pain and confusion and frustration and anger. It made you wonder if God left you. It made you wonder if He was ever with you in the first place.

Or...

Maybe God is hiding Himself from you so that He can speak to your spirit. So He can speak truth to you. Deep truth.

If that's you, I'm going to give you the same advice someone gave me about ten years ago: listen.

Quiet yourself, and listen.

. . . .

That's exactly what Vickie told me to do.

"Dugan, you might not feel God, but He is with you and I believe He is speaking to you," she said. "Get a journal and a pen, go sit down, and just say, *Ok God...I'm listening.* And then just listen. Listen and write down what you hear Him saying."

So I did.

I got up from that table in Kansas City with a renewed sense of hope.

God is with me…even if I can't feel Him. Not only that, but God might be doing it intentionally because He's talking to me!

The thought put a charge through my spirit and I felt new life and energy as I walked back into the enormous worship service going on in the next room. I suddenly felt not only encouraged but also privileged. God hadn't lost my number! He was doing something purposeful in me! He wants to talk to me!

I went back into the stadium, but I was now oblivious to the music, lights, and thousands of people worshipping at full volume around me. I wasn't jealous of them anymore. I just wanted to listen for God's voice. A voice that might have been speaking to me for the last few years but I'd been too confused and angry to hear. That was about to change.

I squeezed back down the aisle to my seat, between all my friends who had their eyes closed and hands raised. I felt like it was just God and me in that moment. Like I was about to go meet Him for this appointment that we had both been looking forward to for years. I had finally started seeking Him and He was just as excited to be found.

I grabbed my bag, slung it over my shoulder and headed to the back of the room, where I sat down and pulled out a pen.

I opened my notebook to the first blank page, put the pen

at the top of the paper, and prayed a simple prayer. *Ok Lord, I'm listening.*

It reminded me of 1 Samuel 3, when God spoke to Samuel, then just a kid, in the middle of the night. He kept hearing God but couldn't see Him, so Samuel walked into his uncle's room and asked, "You called?"

Eventually, his uncle figured out what was going on and told Samuel to respond, "Speak, Lord, your servant is listening."

So I sat there, listening.

Then I started to write.

And write.

And I didn't stop.

I wrote line after line, and over the course of the following months and years, filled page after page, notebook after notebook, and journal after journal. All with what I sensed God speaking to me when I couldn't feel Him.

Sometimes it was very clear what He was saying, and sometimes it felt very faint. Sometimes I sensed Him saying something simple like "I love you." Sometimes I sensed Him speaking wisdom about some relationship or situation in my life that I had asked for guidance about. Sometimes

I sensed Him telling me to pray for a friend or to pray for myself. Sometimes I sensed Him giving me perspective or insight into a passage of the Bible I was reading. Sometimes it felt like we were in an actual dialogue or conversation. And sometimes, I didn't sense Him saying anything. I just sat there listening for a while.

But the whole time, I never *felt* Him. There was no emotion associated with hearing His voice. It wasn't like the clouds parted and I heard Morgan Freeman's baritone voice booming through the sunrays. But I did sense God speaking to me.

Having gone through an intense season of hurt and loneliness and confusion, it was in Kansas City that I began to understand something: **I am never alone.**

Ever.

No matter what I feel or see or experience, the truth is that God is always with me.

For the first time in as long as I could remember, I began to feel a deep sense of longing for God. A longing I'd felt my whole life in some form or another, but that I hadn't paid attention to in years. In fact, I realized that part of the reason I had been so angry with God during the previous few years was because I missed Him!

When I couldn't feel Him, I assumed He'd left me and that

I was now separated from the God I had grown up following and worshipping. It felt like my best friend moved to China without saying goodbye (I think God has a vacation home there). But as much as I wanted to just walk away from the God I thought deserted me, something inside me knew I couldn't.

Now that I had read this story of the disciples on the road to Emmaus and seen that God was with them even when they didn't know it, I started to realize: *God has been with me this whole time, even though I couldn't feel Him.*

Not only that, but He was speaking to me!

That is a life changing thought.
Now came the hard part: learning how to listen to God in my everyday life, all while still not feeling Him.

CHAPTER SIX

LISTEN

If you don't feel God with you, that doesn't mean He's not speaking to you. In fact, it could be *because* He's speaking to you. Speaking truth to you. Truth about yourself, about your life, about Himself, about your future, about His love for you, about the people around you, about anything. Heart to heart. Spirit to spirit. Sometimes He might just tell you He loves you. Sometimes He might give you understanding about a passage of Scripture. Sometimes He might challenge you. Sometimes He might help you.

Just keep in mind that hearing God doesn't always mean feeling Him.

He will be gracious if you ask for help.
   He will surely respond to the sound of your cries.
Your own ears will hear him.
   Right behind you a voice will say,
"This is the way you should go,"

whether to the right or to the left.
– Isaiah 30:19b; 21

It's so interesting that this verse specifies that sometimes when we hear God, it will be "behind" us. Why behind us? **Because sometimes we might hear Him, even when we can't see Him.**

Honestly, most of the time that's difficult. Especially at first. It's not like the first time I sat down to listen for God's voice after Kansas City I heard Him immediately. It actually took practice to learn the process and discipline of quieting my mind enough to hear Him.

Why does God talk like this? Why doesn't He rent out billboard space or a Facebook ad? Unfortunately, I don't know. Here's what I do know: shouting can cause people to tune out, but whispering can cause them to lean in.

Whispering forces us to listen harder.

When you're in your friend's basement and they're quietly telling you about the struggles in their family, you're locked in on their every word.

When you're crying and your parent holds you and whispers "It's gonna be okay," your heart soaks up their voice.

When your boyfriend or girlfriend is about to get out of the car after a date and says, "I had a great time with you tonight," your ears feel like they're going to explode, even though nobody outside of three feet could have heard it.

If someone has to shout, it too often means that either what they have to say isn't very important or that the person receiving the message isn't a good listener. Or both. But shouting won't improve the message or make anyone better at listening. If something is important, and if the receiver is listening carefully, then a quiet voice and even some pauses and silences are far more effective.

That's why there's no such thing as "shouting sweet nothings" into someone's ear. A man who is in love might shout "I LOVE THIS WOMAN!" from the rooftops or Oprah's couch, but a man who truly means it will firmly and softly say it in front of his bride on their wedding day.

We often think of God's voice as one that thunders over the mountains and shakes our whole bodies. Obviously, God is powerful. But the Bible indicates that His preferred mode of communication is more of a whisper than a shout.

"Go out and stand before me on the mountain," the LORD told him. And as Elijah stood there, the LORD passed by, and a mighty windstorm hit the mountain. It was such a terrible blast that the rocks were torn loose, but the LORD was not in the wind. After the wind there was an earthquake, but the LORD was not in the earthquake. And after the earthquake there was a fire, but the LORD was not in the fire. And after the fire there was the sound of a gentle whisper.

When Elijah heard it, he wrapped his face in his cloak and went out and stood at the entrance of the cave. And a voice said, "What are you doing here, Elijah?"
– 1 Kings 19:11-13

God's voice is a "gentle whisper."

The Hebrew word for "whisper" is *demama*, which means "calm."

God's voice has strength, not volume. It is calm, not loud.

....

After Kansas City, as I started to practice listening for God's voice, I quickly realized my biggest problem was that I was used to living in a world of noise!

Everything around me was loud and trying to get louder to compete with the racket. And this made it challenging to learn how to listen to God's whisper.

First of all, there was literal noise that I had to practice turning down—television, friends, internet, my cell phone, video games. Plus maybe the hardest one of all: music.

As I started to practice listening to God, I needed to discipline myself to turn it all down.

Jesus said, *"But when you pray, go away by yourself, shut the*

door behind you, and pray to your Father in private."
– Matthew 6:6.

This doesn't mean we shouldn't pray in public or with other people. It also doesn't mean the only way to pray is by shaving the top of our heads and wearing a coffee-colored robe. Instead, Jesus is teaching us that prayer, a personal conversation between us and God, is best done in private, without all the noise and distractions of the world around us.

I had to learn and practice how to literally turn down the world around me. I had to step out of my normal day-to-day noisy life to find the necessary silence to listen.

But then I realized that turning down the outside noise was the easy part. The more difficult part was learning how to quiet all the inner noise.

Have you ever heard inside my head? That party is *loud,* and I imagine yours is probably no different. If you've ever accidentally found yourself sitting quietly without any distractions (a rare accident these days), then you know how much noise your mind can make. It's like all of your thoughts come rushing to the surface, thrilled to finally have some space where they can run around. Music lyrics, movie quotes, to-do lists, conversation rehearsals, Homer Simpson quotes, and trying to memorize the "Single Ladies" dance are just a fraction of the things I find myself thinking about when it gets quiet. And these don't just automatically shut down when attempting to hear God.

As a student, whenever I tried listening to God, my brain suddenly went all "Scarlett Johansson in *Lucy*" on me. Hyper drive. Crazy. I'd be thinking about my day, about a conversation I had the night before, about what I wanted for lunch, about why my pinky toe itched, about a Travis Barker drum beat I wanted to learn, about how much I was dreading Algebra later, about that annoying thing my sister did, about maybe sleeping over at my best friend's house that weekend, about how that burp tasted like eggs, about chores I had to do, about how much chocolate milk I thought I could drink before it came out my eyeballs, about how lucky dogs are that they get to poop in public, about how my butt was asleep, about how I hadn't washed my sheets in a few weeks, about how awesome I was for listening to God...oh wait, I totally wasn't listening at all!

As much of a discipline as it was to turn down all the outside noise, it was an even bigger discipline to turn down all the internal noise. All my thoughts and worries and memories and plans and everything in between were suddenly, as they say in *Spinal Tap*, turned up to eleven when I tried to quiet myself and listen to God!

If you're anything like me (someone who isn't diagnosed, but probably has ADHD), it feels like the quieter it is around me, the louder my mind gets. That's why I love listening to music when I study or write or read, because it gives my spastic brain something to focus on while I think

about whatever task I'm trying to accomplish in front
of me.

At first I thought it was impossible to shut my brain up.

I would sit for an hour trying to listen to God and end up
spending the whole time trying not to think about whatever I was thinking about. And the harder I tried not thinking about what I was thinking about, the more I thought
about not thinking about it. You with me?

So I had to practice, day after day, hour after hour, minute
after minute, learning to quiet my mind. And this is much
easier said than done. But I kept at it because even though I
couldn't feel God, I wanted to hear Him.

Each morning after breakfast, I had a solid hour set aside
before the rest of my day where I would just sit on the
couch in my room and practice listening. I might start by
reading a passage of scripture or play a worship song quietly before turning it off, but then I would spend the majority
of that hour just sitting with my eyes closed.

I sat up so I wouldn't fall asleep (it's possible that happened
once or twice before I learned to not recline while praying).
I kept my eyes closed so I wouldn't be visually distracted
by everything around me. I kept all noise off, even worship
music, so there wouldn't be any outside stimulation to distract me from trying to quiet my heart to listen for God.
And although it took a lot of time and a lot of discipline

and a lot of practice, I slowly started to get better at it.

The key term here is "slowly." Malcolm Gladwell, the best-selling author of *Outliers: The Story of Success*, says it takes about ten-thousand hours of doing something to become an expert at it. Meaning it would probably take at least half that to become somewhat good at something. So, it's not like I could spend one hour listening for God and expect to become a master at it. It took time. But the more I practiced, the easier it got.

In 2 Corinthians 5:10, Paul talks about how we, as Christ followers, aren't battling a physical battle but a spiritual one. He uses this language about our thoughts and teaches us to "take every thought captive and make it obedient to Christ."

I thought of this verse a lot while I was learning how to quiet my mind. It would frequently feel like I had all of these thoughts swirling around my head, like a swarm of Golden Snitches that even Harry Potter couldn't catch. And every time one of these thoughts would hit the front of my brain, I would quickly grab it, and surrender it to God.

I'd suddenly think, *I wonder if I could do a back flip off my bed.* Then I'd pray something like, "God, that's stupid and I'd probably break my neck, so I surrender this thought to you."

Or I would think, *If my best friend became a zombie, would I be able to kill him?* Then I'd pray, "God, that's another stupid thought, because of course I'd be able to kill him, and I surrender this thought to You."

And the more I practiced this, the easier it got. And the easier it got, the more clearly I started hearing God's voice.

Jesus even talks about the practice of recognizing God's voice:

"The one who enters by the gate is the shepherd of the sheep. The gatekeeper opens the gate for him, and the sheep listen to his voice. He calls his own sheep by name and leads them out. When he has brought out all his own, he goes on ahead of them, and his sheep follow him because they know his voice." – John 10:2-4

Jesus is our Shepherd and we are His sheep. We can know His voice, but it will take practice to discern His voice and then hear it clearly.

I believe there are three main voices we can hear in our spirits: the voice of God, our own thoughts, and the lies of Satan. Each of these can be influenced by countless other voices such as family, media, friends or culture, but these are the three main categories of what speaks to us internally. And as radically different as all these sound, it can be shockingly difficult to discern between each of them.

This is why knowing the truth, God's truth, is so much more important than what we feel or even what we think. Because knowing God's truth is the only way we can discern His voice amid all the noise.

We're taught to trust what we feel, which is why relationships fail, why happiness can't be bought, and why so many students walk away from God. Emotions just don't hold up. Eventually, they always fail.

But truth doesn't fail. God doesn't fail.

Nobody would ever say "I don't feel love for my wife so I must not be married" or "I don't feel like going to a movie so I must hate movies" or "I don't feel hungry right now so I must have never have to eat food!" Emotions come and go, but we know they don't change the truth. Nor should we let them change our faith in God.

The truth of God's presence is bigger than what we feel. He is not bound by our emotions. They don't determine whether or not God is present.

Our emotions are not a trustworthy indication of whether or not God is with us. They are a potential byproduct of His presence, but not a determining factor.

I once heard a pastor who was teaching about healing say, "Seek the Healer, not the healing." So many times, we seek God for what we need or want instead of just seeking God.

When it comes to listening for God's voice, make sure that you're truly seeking after Him and hearing Him, not just what you want to hear Him say. Seek the wisdom-giver, not just the wisdom. Seek the speaker, not just the words. Seek God, not just the feeling of Him.

I'm sure it makes God sad when he's trying to talk to us but we're too concerned with telling Him what we need or want.

. . . .

I have a few pet peeves. One of my biggest pet peeves is when people stand too close behind me in a line. I always wonder if they're in a hurry or if they're there to assassinate me. Another pet peeve I have is salt in chocolate or caramel. I'm serious. Sweet should be sweet and salt should be salty. The day they come out with Sea Salt Cinnamon Toast Crunch, I'm picketing the nearest cereal aisle.

But my biggest pet peeve is when I'm talking to someone who I can tell is not listening—when someone pretends to listen, but is really just waiting for their turn to speak. This usually becomes obvious when the first thing they say when I'm done talking is, "Yeah, for me..."

Unfortunately, this is something I do way too often with God. So many times when praying to God, it's all about me. I'm not sure if this is a pet peeve of God's, but I'm sure He's disappointed when I start every prayer by saying, "Hey

God! Okay, so for me..."

Of course it's not bad to talk to God, but I think it makes God sad when we miss 50 percent of what prayer should be: listening.

So stop missing it.

Listen.

Keep in mind, there's no wrong way to do it and definitely no "one right way" to listen to God. It's going to look different for each person, but here are a few steps to get you started:

STEP ONE: **BE ALONE**

This doesn't mean that you have to hike up to a monastery like Bruce Wayne in *Batman Begins*, but it's important to have some element of solitude as you try and hear God's voice.

For me this was sitting alone in my room with the door closed.

For you this might be going to a park and sitting outside in nature.

It could be putting on headphones at a coffee shop or library.

It could be driving your car somewhere and just sitting in a parking lot or at a nature preserve.

It could be sitting at your kitchen, in your closet, on your bed, or on your back deck.

It could be standing, pacing, or hanging by your ankles from the ceiling in your garage... actually that last one is creepy, don't do that.

The point is, it doesn't matter! Just find a place where you can be alone to listen to God.

STEP TWO: **ELIMINATE OUTSIDE NOISE**

I'm someone who loves and needs background music all the time. But when it comes to listening for God's voice, I need to make sure it's quiet so I can hear my thoughts and continually surrender the distracting ones to God. Like I said, there's no wrong way to do this, so if you feel like some background worship or Sufjan Stevens helps, then go for it. The point is to be able to push everything aside and focus on God and His voice. So find the environment that best suits that goal.

STEP THREE: **SURRENDER YOUR THOUGHTS TO GOD**

When thoughts begin to distract you from listening to God, get in the habit of surrendering them to Him. Don't dwell on the thought. Just take it and pray, "God, I surrender this thought to You and am listening for Your voice." This is pretty difficult at first, but I promise that the more you practice, the better you will get at it.

Plus, bonus, this is a great practice for life overall. It's helpful to exercise the muscle of surrendering our thoughts to God so we can also surrender thoughts of gossip or lust or fear to Him in other situations (2 Corinthians 10:5).

STEP FOUR: **WRITE IT DOWN**

I filled so many journals with what I sensed God was speaking to me, and it's been a huge blessing to be able to go back and read them and see the journey God brought me through.

Another reason it's good to write things down is to help sort and clarify what you are hearing. Sometimes you'll read something you wrote down and realize that it actually might have been your own thought instead of something God was saying. Often, you'll figure that out when you incorporate the next step.

STEP FIVE: **COMPARE IT TO THE BIBLE**

The best filter for what we sense God saying to us is Scripture. For example, if you sense God saying "I love you," that would be true, since the Bible is clear about God's love for us. But sensing something like "I want you to punch that baby bird in the face" would not be from God, since the

Bible talks about kindness and honoring creation. And for real, don't punch birds.

STEP SIX: TELL SOMEONE

Listening to God isn't some secret that you have to keep to yourself. Talk to people about it! Your parents or friends or youth pastors or small group leaders or whoever! It's not only exciting to tell people what you sense God saying to you, but it can also be super helpful if there's something you need clarity about.

In his book *Hiddenness and Manifestation,* Graham Cooke, the author I mentioned earlier in chapter four, gives us a prayer to use when listening to God: "I know You, Lord, You're here somewhere. I'm just going to wait until You come or wait until You speak. I know You're doing something. I haven't figured out what it is yet, but I'm just going to wait because I know You."

I'd encourage you to try it until you get more comfortable with listening for God's voice. I know it helped me a lot.

. . . .

I am a huge fan of golf. I love watching it live and on TV. I love reading about it, and I love playing it. Over the years, I've gotten better little by little—and most of that has come from understanding my swing and what I need to change to make it better.

But whenever I adjust something about my swing or stance or grip, it feels weird. There have been so many times when I've been playing and my swing felt awesome, but as I look up, I see my ball making a beeline for the woods or nearest body of water. Then there are other times when my swing has felt awkward, but my shot is long and straight. What gives?

Well, as shocking as this might be, I don't have a perfect golf swing (for that, watch Rory McIlroy). I swing the way I do because it feels comfortable, even if the result causes my ball to end up in a bird's nest or somewhere in North Dakota.

Just because it feels natural for me doesn't mean it's the best option. In fact, there are times when I know I'm doing something wrong and need to change, but every time I do, it feels weird. Which is why I have to practice it over and over again until the right thing starts to feel, well, right.

And believe me, the practice of listening for God will feel weird at first. And it is going to take a lot practice to get comfortable. It's gonna feel funny to sit silently somewhere just listening, especially when you first start or when you aren't hearing God say anything.

But the more you practice, the more it will start to feel a little more comfortable. Until one day, when you'll be able to go through your everyday life and constantly be listening to God. When you go to school or work, when you're talking to a friend, when you're stressed or angry or afraid or overjoyed, you'll have gotten so good at listening for God's voice, it just becomes natural for you to do so.

. . . .

Since God's voice tends to be a whisper, it can be hard to hear it unless we're listening. Because of what I learned at that cafeteria table in Kansas City, I avoided one of the greatest potential tragedies for mankind: when God speaks, but no one notices.

So, listen.

CHAPTER SEVEN

CSI CHRISTIANITY

My wife Lindsay is an incredibly talented artist. A couple years after we got married, she was down in our basement painting when I decided to be the greatest husband in the history of husbands and do some laundry. OK fine, I was out of underwear.

So I gathered up our clothes and sheets before heading down to the basement, where our washer and dryer were located. Lindsay was just a few feet away in the corner of the room with all her art supplies. Her back was to me and she was painting her heart out. She was wearing a cute outfit of sweat pants, an old Chicago Cubs T-shirt, and some sheepskin boots. She had her hair up in a bun and her headphones were blasting music. She was humming along, eying her work, and being adorable.

As I stood there, feeling an overwhelming sense of love and attraction for my wife, she turned to get more paint and saw me out of the corner of her eye—a tall, shadowy figure standing silently behind her in our basement.

She screamed, dropped her paintbrush, and started sobbing.

"What are you doing!?!" she said (yelled) to me.

"Oh no, no, no! I was just coming to do the laundry and was watching you for a second!" I said, trying to calm her down.

"You scared me to death!" she said, still crying.

Well, needless to say, my romantic movie moment was a little ruined, and she gave me half-serious dirty looks for the rest of the day.

We laugh about it now, but here's my point: her fear, while real, was totally irrational. She knew I was home. We lived in a safe neighborhood. There wasn't anybody else in the house. I was just trying to wash my undies.

It might be a silly example, but it shows why it can be so unwise to base our decisions and beliefs on immediate emotions and not larger truth.

For one, emotions are fragile. They can change in a split second. Not only that, but emotions are also completely out of our control. Someone can't sit down to watch the movie *Paranormal Activity* with me and say, "Just don't feel scared, okay?" You can tell your love-struck friend to stop being obsessed with Bruno Mars, but she'll say something like, "I can't! He's so gorgeous and he just *gets* me." And that's part of what makes emotions so powerful. We can't control them; we just feel them as they come.

A large part of life is not going to be emotional. As we've talked about, emotions can be great but should not be any kind of foundation for our life or decisions.

There are amazing moments in life when we experience a surge of emotion: a first kiss, a scary movie, sky diving, winning a championship, our wedding day, the birth of a child, etc. All of these are moments when we experience a high degree of emotion, which is great!

But the other 98 percent of life isn't like that. The majority of life isn't a highly emotional experience. And that's okay. That's normal!

And it's also normal in our relationship with God. There might be moments of intense emotion with God, but the majority of the time our walk with God isn't going to be a highly emotional experience. Nor should it be.

Learning how to follow God even when we can't feel Him means learning how to follow God despite our emotions, not because of them.

We need to learn how to follow God in the emotionally normal, the emotionally mundane.

A healthy marriage is like this, too. As two people meet, date, get engaged, and get married, their relationship is filled with incredibly strong emotional moments. But eventually the emotions taper off and become less intense. This isn't a sign that the relationship is dying; it's simply the reality of life.

But here's the important part: learning to live life in the emotionally normal can be amazing! Because of the culture around us, we tend to think that an emotional high is the goal for our lives and that anything short of that means we're missing it. But truthfully, we don't need emotion to experience the joy and power of life.

By far, my favorite moments with Lindsay aren't the emotionally charged ones. They're things like playing a card game together at her sister's wedding, laughing at the same time at a television show, getting a random kiss because I filled her car up with gas unexpectedly, road trips together, breakfast-for-dinner nights, Netflix marathons, and so much more. These are some of my favorite things about my marriage, not just the moments when my emotions were at their peak.

If I were to enter into my marriage with an expectation of constant emotional highs, it would be really unhealthy. It would be exhausting. I'd have unrealistic expectations, and

I'd make her feel awful when she couldn't meet them. I'd probably cause a lot of damage to us both. While my wife and I treasure the emotional-high moments in our relationship (dating, vacations, anniversaries), there is also joy and life and depth in the day-to-day, learning-and-growing-together moments.

And following God in the emotionally normal doesn't mean having a faith that is devoid of power or passion or joy.

It means having a faith that is not shaken by the swing of emotion.

It means building our lives on truth and nothing else.

It means knowing a personal God, regardless of what we feel.

And how do you do that? You look for evidence.

. . . .

One of my favorite TV shows is *CSI*. The original one, not the one with the over-dramatic redhead always taking his sunglasses off like he's God's gift to people who like watching other people take their sunglasses off. Also not the one with Lieutenant Dan. I mean the original one. The one with stellar lead characters played by the likes of William Petersen, Laurence "Morpheus" Fishburne, and Sir Ted Danson.

The show has gone through its cheesy phases, but it's one of the only shows I've stuck with since the beginning, along with *Breaking Bad* (good decision) and *Lost* (terrible decision).

I usually make the mistake of watching a DVR'd episode of *CSI* during lunch or dinner, which is unfortunate because each episode usually starts with a murder that's often accompanied by fake blood and gross sound effects as they dissect the body to find out the cause of death. I haven't eaten spaghetti in years.

In any type of show like *CSI* or *Law & Order* or any good mystery movie, there's one thing that the entire episode is usually centered around. It's the thing that the police look for, it's what the specialists gather, and it's the determining factor on who is innocent and who is guilty. (Tip: The villian is almost always the nicest character you meet in the beginning of the episode, right after the murder scene—the wife, the sweet old guy who lives next door, the pet bunny, etc.)

I'm talking about evidence.

Each cop show or murder mystery is centered around the gathering of evidence to determine the truth about a person or situation. Because evidence leads to truth.

These days there are men and women released from prison because the newest forms of technology enable us to gather evidence that we couldn't before. Things like DNA, finger-prints, and facial recognition are all part of the evidence we now use to figure out the truth behind a crime.

In the same way, instead of relying on emotions or external perception, let's check out the evidence in these scripture verses and discover truth that we can put our faith in.

EVIDENCE #1

Then Moses called for Joshua, and as all Israel watched, he said to to him, "Be strong and courageous! For you will lead these people into the land that the Lord swore to their an-cestors he would give them. You are the one who will divide it among them as their grants of land. Do not be afraid or discouraged, for the Lord will personally go ahead of you. He will be with you; he will neither fail you nor abandon you."
– Deuteronomy 31:7-8

This is a promise Moses gives to Joshua, telling him that he will become Israel's next leader. A powerful word from a guy who God used in so many ways, from helping free the Israelites from slavery in Egypt to parting the Red Sea, to writing most (if not all) of the first five books of the Bible. Interestingly enough, the next book of the Bible has God saying almost the exact same thing to Joshua directly.

EVIDENCE #2

"This is my command—be strong and courageous! Do not

be afraid or discouraged. For the Lord your God is with you wherever you go." – Joshua 1:9

Right after Moses died, God chose Joshua to begin leading His people. The last thing God said to Joshua in this passage is in verse 9, where the Lord commands (not asks or suggests) that Joshua be strong and courageous. What was the source of Joshua's strength and courage? The fact that God was with him *wherever he went.*

Things probably got difficult, leadership was hard, and there were times when Joshua might have wondered if God was with him at all. In those moments, God commanded him to find His strength in the truth that he was never alone, that God was with him always. Because just like us, Joshua's success wasn't a matter of Joshua's talent or gifts or ability. It was most significantly dependent on God's presence with him, which God promised would be constant.

EVIDENCE #3

For he himself has said, "I will never leave you nor forsake you." So we may boldly say: "The Lord is my helper; I will not fear. What can man do to me?" – Hebrews 13:5-6

God's presence is our strength. When fear raises it's ugly, zombie-like head, when we experience the pain of life, when we walk through shadows of death—our strength comes from God's presence, which is always with us, no matter what we feel.

EVIDENCE #4

One of my favorite Biblical stories is the account of Joseph's life. Not because he had a multi-colored hipster jacket thousands of years before *Portlandia* became a thing, but because of his amazing story.

He went through this perilous journey with so many ups and downs, all by God's design.

You've probably heard it before: Out of a family with twelve boys, Joseph was his dad's favorite. One way Joseph's dad showed this was by giving him that colorful coat. In ancient times, colors weren't super easy to make or come by, so having a coat that wasn't Lame Beige or EndLess Desert Sand Brown was kind of a big deal. Because he was so favored by his dad, his brothers were jealous and hated Joseph. Seems about right (I'm pretty sure my parents like my sister better too). So they beat him up, stole his coat, and sold him into slavery.

As a slave, through hard work and being a man of great character, Joseph got promoted to head of his master's household. He was trusted, given responsibility, and not mistreated. But then Joseph was falsely accused of trying to have sex with Potiphar's wife, and he was thrown into prison.

Joseph went from head of a household to prisoner...for something he didn't do. But he was still a man of God and of great character, so he just kept on living life. And eventually, through some crazy circumstances, he ended up interpreting a dream for Pharaoh, the leader of Egypt. He then made Joseph the second in command leader over all of Egypt!

If you were to look at a scale of how good or bad Joseph's ife was, it might look something like this:

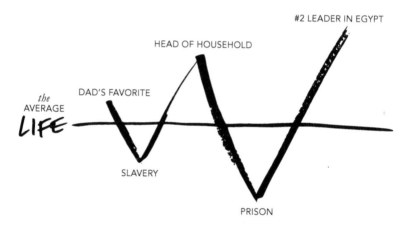

As you can see, Joseph went from a life slightly above average to one slightly below it, then jumped to an even better life, followed by a drop to one way below it. Finally his life rose all the way to a point where he was the right-hand man to the leader of the most powerful nation in the world at that time! Crazy, right?

Yes it is.

But the most amazing part of Joseph's story is that, aside from a prophetic dream that Joseph had at the beginning of his story, there wasn't any evidence of God's presence in Joseph's life. When Joseph's life was awesome, the Bible doesn't talk about God's face appearing or voice speaking blessing to Joseph. More importantly, when Joseph was sold into slavery or unjustly thrown in prison, the Bible doesn't talk about Joseph feeling encouraged by God's presence or an angel showing up to tell him it was going to be okay and that God was there.

It's possible that something like that happened, but the sense that I get from reading Joseph's story is that throughout everything he went though, he didn't feel or sense God.

When things were great and when things were terrible, Joseph didn't sense God was with him.

Yet when we read his story, it's so obvious that God *was* with him! God was clearly orchestrating this incredible journey, all of which led to Joseph becoming a powerful leader and saving the lives of millions of people (including his family and brothers) during a huge famine.

While it's not clearly stated, it appears that Joseph went through this entire process without feeling or sensing God's presence. But God was there. God was with him. God gave him dreams to encourage him, the strength to resist temptation, and the power to interpret the meaning of other people's dreams. Where other stories feature God calling in the middle of the night, or closing the mouths of lions, or sending angels, Joseph's story seems to be strangely empty of God's presence. But in retrospect, you can you see how it all worked together, how God was present in every detail and moment and twist in the story.

What if our lives looked the same way? We go through life's twists and turns, all without feeling God, only to look back one day and see that God was totally part of every aspect of our lives.

Evidence.

Throughout scripture, we see the same thing again and again: God's fingerprints were all over people's lives—especially when they couldn't feel Him.

CHAPTER EIGHT

REMEMBER

I don't have a great memory.

I can be a good memorizer when it comes to funny things Will Ferrell says or the lyrics to Smash Mouth songs, but when it comes to remembering things in the moment, I'm pretty terrible. I'm an expert at using terms like "man," "dude," "bro," and "pal" in an endearing way when I can't remember someone's name, which is…always.

But as bad as I am at remembering names, there are certain things that have stuck with me over the years. I usually can't remember the three things I need from the grocery store, but I have a crystal clear memory of a Panera Bread commercial I heard on the radio once over ten years ago. I usually can't remember what I walked in the kitchen for, but I remember the code to unlock every level of Sonic the Hedgehog for Sega Genesis (it's UP-DOWN-LEFT-

RIGHT-HOLD "A"-START…you're welcome).

One thing that has always stuck with me is a teaching I heard several years ago at a church in downtown Chicago from a guy named Jon, who was the worship leader for my high school ministry. That morning Jon taught about Psalm 77.

Most of the Psalms are uplifting and full of beautiful imagery of how wonderful and loving God is. But not Psalm 77. It was written by a guy named Asaph, and here's how it starts:

I cry out to God; yes, I shout.
  Oh, that God would listen to me!
When I was in deep trouble,
  I searched for the Lord.
All night long I prayed, with hands lifted toward heaven,
  but my soul was not comforted.
I think of God, and I moan,
  overwhelmed with longing for his help.
You don't let me sleep.
  I am too distressed even to pray!
I think of the good old days,
  long since ended,
when my nights were filled with joyful songs.
  I search my soul and ponder the difference now.
Has the Lord rejected me forever?
  Will he never again be kind to me?
Is his unfailing love gone forever?

Have his promises permanently failed?
Has God forgotten to be gracious?
*   Has he slammed the door on his compassion?*
And I said, "This is my fate;
*   the Most High has turned his hand against me."*

Look how honest Asaph is with God. Consider lines like "I searched for the Lord...but my soul was not comforted" or "You don't let me sleep...I'm too distressed to pray!" or "Has the Lord rejected me forever? Is His love gone forever? Has God forgotten to be gracious?"

Reading those, it's easy to think, *Um...is this okay to be in the Bible? Can he say that? Did this sneak past the editing team or something?*

Isn't the Bible supposed to be all about love and rainbows and unicorns (before they were late getting on the ark)? Isn't everything in the Bible about God supposed to be about His love and grace and peace?

But the beginning of Psalm 77 isn't positive at all! It's written to God in a raw and honest way. Asaph is being totally real with God about what he's feeling, without trying to sugarcoat anything or put on a false, happy face.

Asaph is clearly going through an extremely painful time in his life, but whenever he cries out to God, he doesn't see or feel or hear anything. He feels like all of God's love and grace has run out, that God has forgotten about him, that

God has rejected him. He can't even sleep because of the overwhelming struggle and pain.

Despite Asaph's attempts to reach out and seek after God, God doesn't seem to be there.

So why didn't this passage get edited out? Because God isn't afraid of us being totally honest with Him.

We sometimes think that we have to edit ourselves when talking to God. We think our prayers have to be filled with big Christian words and all positive things, no matter what. We think, even during the worst day possible, we should make sure all we pray about are the things we're thankful for and how awesome life is…even when it isn't.

But God is big enough for our honesty. In fact, God would prefer us to be honest with Him.

For one thing, He knows how we're feeling even when we lie about it. But more than that, He desires us to be honest with Him. He's big enough to take our doubt and pain and anger and frustration and confusion and hatred. We're not going to scare Him away or tick Him off. Remember, He's always with us and there's nothing we can do to change that.

If anything, being brutally honest with God, especially about the things that are less than positive, is going to be more honoring and draw us closer to Him. We might think that faking happiness is what God wants, but when we fake it, we put up a wall between us and Him.

And it's only by being honest with Him that we can begin to discover the truth.

I experience this a lot with my wife.

I tend to be more of an introverted, private person, so I'm constantly in this process of learning how to communicate well with Lindsay. But she is super wise and can always tell when something is bothering me.

There have been times when, sensing something is bothering me, she will look at me and ask, "What's wrong?"

"Nothing!" I'll say quickly and defensively, making it pretty clear that something is definitely wrong.

"You sure?" she'll patiently ask.

"Yeah, I'm fine." (I'm not.)

This might happen once or twice more, but eventually, my dishonesty will build up and we'll get in a fight, or I'll finally come clean with what's bothering me, and after we work it out, Lindsay will lovingly say, "Why didn't you just tell me you were mad from the beginning? It could have saved us a lot of time and frustration."

My awesome comeback is usually something like, "Um…
I don't know."

Because it was stupid! I should have just been honest with
her from the beginning! Pretending everything is okay
actually ends up causing us more difficulty. Pushing down
my feelings only increases their weight and pressure, like
pushing a beach ball under water. And Lindsay knows
something is wrong anyway, leading her to wonder why I
don't trust her with how I'm feeling and don't want to share
my heart with her.

I've learned it's the same with God. He knows what's going
on inside of us anyway. But more importantly, He wants us
to be honest with Him. He's not afraid of our honesty, and
our honesty isn't going to affect His love for us. He literally cannot love us any less or any more, regardless of how
honest we are with Him.

**God would rather us authentically say "I hate you" than
falsely say "I love you."**

Because once we say "I hate you," then we can begin the
process of discovering why we hate God—the root of our
hate being anger, the root of our anger being pain. And
what is the root of pain? I think most of the anger we have
toward God can be boiled down to feeling like He abandoned us (or someone close to us) either for a season or in
situation that we needed Him. That was the root of Asaph's
pain. It was the root of mine. And the only path toward

healing and truth is to first be honest about that feeling.

So if you can't feel God, tell Him! Be honest and real with Him about it. Tell Him it sucks. Tell Him you're angry. Tell Him it's confusing. Tell Him what it feels like.

Be honest. It's what God wants.

But don't stop there.

You'll notice that Psalm 77 doesn't end at verse 10. There's this major transition in verse 11 that starts, "But then I recall…"

Check it out:

But then I recall all you have done, O Lord;
*   I remember your wonderful deeds of long ago.*
They are constantly in my thoughts.
*   I cannot stop thinking about your mighty works.*
O God, your ways are holy.
*   Is there any god as mighty as you?*
You are the God of great wonders!
*   You demonstrate your awesome power among*
*   the nations.*
By your strong arm, you redeemed your people,
*   the descendants of Jacob and Joseph.*

When the Red Sea saw you, O God,
*   its waters looked and trembled!*

The sea quaked to its very depths.
The clouds poured down rain;
  the thunder rumbled in the sky.
  Your arrows of lightning flashed.
Your thunder roared from the whirlwind;
  the lightning lit up the world!
  The earth trembled and shook.
Your road led through the sea,
  your pathway through the mighty waters—
  a pathway no one knew was there!
You led your people along that road like a flock of sheep,
  with Moses and Aaron as their shepherds.

There's this real important shift that happens in Psalm 77. Asaph went from brutal honesty about his circumstances to remembering what God had already done. He expressed the far less-than-perfect things he was thinking and feeling, but didn't stay stuck there. After he was honest with God, he remembered the truth of who God was from his own experience.

Be honest with God…but then remember the truth.

Be painfully authentic; hold nothing back. Be raw and real with God. But then choose to remember the past when you didn't feel this way. Be honest about not feeling God, but then remember a time when you did feel Him.

Because the past can be an encouragement to our present.

Everything in life is seasonal. There are seasons when life is great and seasons when it is difficult. There are seasons when we can feel God and seasons when we can't. And for those seasons when we can't feel God, an important part of getting through it is remembering those times when we did feel God's presence. By remembering those times, we can remind ourselves of the truth, despite our current emotions.

A baseball player in a hitting slump needs to remember a time when he was batting .320 to remind him that he *can* hit, despite all current evidence to the contrary, and to focus on whatever mechanics will help him get back to hitting better.

Couples in a struggling marriage are sometimes advised to remember times from early in their relationship, to remind them why they loved each other and how they used to show that love. This helps them remember the greater story of their relationship, which trumps the present difficulty.

Because the same God we felt in the past is still with us. He's still real and present and alive and *with us*. Even if we can't feel Him right now. And just because we can't feel Him right then isn't an indication that He's never been there or isn't right now.

In her book *Faith is Not a Feeling,* Ney Bailey talks about her process of learning that God's truth isn't determined by her emotions. And when the two seemed to contradict each other, she could always trust God's Word over her own feelings.

"I began to realize that this kind of response to my feelings gave me the freedom both to be honest with God about my feelings and to choose to believe God's Word when my feelings contradicted His promises," Bailey writes. "Thousands of times my prayers have begun, 'Lord, I feel…, but, Lord, Your Word says…'"

When doubt comes, we can choose to remember a time when we had no doubt, and believe in the truth, rather than what we feel at the present moment of time.

It might go something like this:

God, I can't feel You right now and I hate it. I'm so angry! I keep asking and asking but get nothing back from You. It feels like You evaporated from my life at a time when I need You most. I don't understand.

But I'm going to choose to remember when I could sense You. I remember feeling you close to me during that worship song on last year's retreat. I remember hearing Your voice when I was praying on the bus in eighth grade. I remember feeling your presence when my small group leader was praying for me.

I don't understand what's going on now, but I will remember those times when I knew You were with me, and I choose to believe that You're with me now, even though it doesn't feel like it.

To help with this, I'm going to give you an exercise that I learned at that Sunday morning church service in Chicago. In fact, I still have the piece of paper I did this with in my Bible.

Take a piece of paper and draw a horizontal line across the middle. In the top portion, write the words "BE HONEST." In the bottom portion, write "REMEMBER."

Then write honest things to God in the top section, followed by things you remember about God in the bottom section. Try it out on the next couple pages.

BE HONEST

REMEMBER

How did it go? If it was challenging, don't sweat. It will take some practice. We're so used to basing our emotions on what's right in front of us that sometimes it will take time to get in the habit of remembering truth from the past. So pat yourself on the back (or ask a friend if you're prone to pulling muscles) and try again tomorrow.

I once heard Pete Wilson, founder and pastor of Cross Point Church, say, "Don't doubt in the dark what God has told you in the light." And nowhere is that better exampled than in Psalm 77. Be brutally honest with God, but then remember.

Maybe you're struggling with remembering times when you knew God was with you. But just like Asaph, you can also look at the truth based on others' experiences. You can lean on the big story of God's faithfulness to His people.

If you think about it, our whole faith is built on one practice: remembering. In order for us to have meaning for our present or hope for our future, we must first remember what God has done in the past. Unfortunately, human beings are prone to forgetting things, which is why people in the Bible were always building piles of rocks and sticking things in the sand and writing things on tablets and having feasts on certain days—so that when God did something important or showed up in an important way, they wouldn't forget.

What do you normally do when you want to remember something?

I sometimes try telling Siri to remind me. But then after a frustrating ten minutes of saying, "Remind me to call Steve's cell" into the phone and hearing her repeat back, "Remind me to fall in a sleeve of bells," I give up and forget to call Steve.

To remember something important, we write it down on a piece of paper or our hand. We send ourselves an e-mail or text. We put reminders in our calendars. We tell people around us, "Hey, can you remind me to…" We set alarms and put things around the house so we see them.

I'm totally an "out of sight, out of mind" kind of person, so I have to do this with almost everything. I have to put my wallet by the back door so I don't forget it on the way to my car. I have to send myself emails to remind myself to send an email. I have to set my phone alarm to remind me to charge my wireless headphones. Linds gets so annoyed at all the notes I keep scattered around the house. But if I don't put reminders where I can see them, I'll forget! I have to take practical steps to make sure that if (when) my memory fails me or I start to get distracted, I will remember something important.

In those moments and seasons when we can't feel God, but we know and choose to believe in the truth that He is with us, we need to remind ourselves that He is there by any means necessary.

There is no wrong way to do this! There are endless tips for reminding yourself of the truth, so find out what works best for you.

Write yourself Post-it notes that you leave in your room or on your mirror or in your locker.

Change your phone background to say "Never Alone," or have a Bible verse like Deuteronomy 31:8 or Psalm 16:8 on it. (Head to NeverAloneShop.com to download free "Never Alone" phone backgrounds!).

Send yourself texts and emails.

Or better yet, team up with a friend and send each other reminders throughout the day that God is with you.

Set your daily alarm to remind you that you are never alone.

Memorize Joshua 1:9 or Hebrews 13:5-6.

Anything!

. . . .

When I really want to remember something, I get a tattoo.

I currently have eight.

I'm not going to make any kind of theological or moral statement about tattoos. I think it's a personal choice for every person. But I've always used tattoos as a way of marking significant, life-long beliefs or truths that are a part of my life.

I only get tattoos of things that I know will be a part of me forever. Something like my faith and relationship with God that I will never walk away from. Also things like my marriage, my kids, and significant truths from the Bible that I've learned are all part of the ink on my pasty white skin.

I do have certain rules about getting tattoos: I can only get something that has significant meaning (no offense to those of you with birds, 90s bands, or Tinker Bell tattoos) and I also have to want a specific tattoo for at least two years before I get it.

My first tattoo was a wooden cross sticking into my skin to represent Galatians 2:20. The verse says, "I have been crucified with Christ and I no longer live but Christ lives in me." I wanted to mark the fact that I had chosen to receive Jesus' forgiveness for my sins and am in the process of dying to my self and submitting to Him, who was now in me.

I got a tattoo to represent the Holy Spirit's power and one to represent God's fatherly love for me. I got my wife's name over my heart and my daughter's name on my ribs. I have a tattoo of my wedding ring and one to represent the spiritual warfare I face everyday (Ephesians 6:12).

And don't let anybody lie to you. Tattoos hurt. A lot. Granted, I'm kind of a wimp with a low pain tolerance, but anybody who says they don't hurt is just trying to impress you or must not have feeling in their epidermis. Because they hurt. I don't know how a machine with seven needles rapidly stabbing your skin for minutes and hours at a time couldn't be painful. But again, I'm kind of a baby.

For me, however, the pain of getting a tattoo is part of the commitment to what it represents. Considering the pain I'll have to endure is part of the process of deciding whether a tattoo is worth it or not.

One of my tattoos is two words written across my back: "Never Alone."

There are and will be times when I might not feel God, when I might be tempted to think He has left me or isn't with me or even close to me. And when I start to go down that road into fear and uncertainty and insecurity and anger and pain, I want to always have something to remind me of the truth: God is with me, and I am never alone.

Remind yourself of this however you can. God is with you, and you are never alone. Always. Forever. He promises this. And God keeps his promises, even when we don't.

He has not left you. No matter what you feel.

I know the Lord is always with me.
  I will not be shaken, for he is right beside me.
  – Psalm 16:8

CHAPTER NINE

FEAR

Maybe the idea of not emotionally experiencing God isn't okay with you. I get it.

There have been times when I've literally begged God to let me feel His presence. And while my intentions were good, my request was a little misguided.

Why? Because the single most common emotion associated with God's presence is fear.

That's correct. Fear.

The more I've searched the Bible for people, accounts, and situations involving someone encountering God, time and time again the main emotional reaction to God's presence is being afraid.

In fact, the most common command in all of Scripture is "Don't be afraid." It's in the Bible three hundred and sixty-six times, one for each day and an extra for leap year!

God's presence is wonderful. His love is powerful. His grace is world changing. It's all so powerful that when God is present, our finite, imperfect, human selves are completely overwhelmed to the point that we feel afraid.

All the big Bible heroes felt fear in God's presence. Abraham, Moses, Noah, Elijah, Peter, John, Paul, Mary, Joseph.

One of my favorite book series is *The Chronicles of Narnia* by C. S. Lewis. There's a quote from the first book that describes Aslan the lion, the Jesus-figure in the series, that says, "He's wild, you know. Not like a tame lion." Throughout the series, Aslan is said to be good, but not tame.

We want God to be safe. We want Him to fit our expectations and not ruffle too many feathers. We want God to make us feel good, to be contained in a box we're comfortable with, and to act in a way that's predictable and explainable.

But that's not God at all. God is good, God is love, but God isn't some divine teddy bear. He is not a tame lion. He's predictably unpredictable.

Have you ever been up close to a lion?

Or any large predator?

I once got to spend a few hours with a police-trained German Shepherd. Obviously a dog is nothing compared to a lion, but it was intense nonetheless. He was trained to bring down criminals two or three times his size.

My friend got to experience this first-hand. As part of a demonstration, he wore a bite-proof suit and took off running. Then, at the right command, this German Shepherd sprinted towards him at full speed, leapt through the air, and clamped his teeth down on my friend's (protected) arm. The dog twisted and pulled in a way that was designed to drop my friend to the ground...which it did, embarrassingly fast. Then the trainer called out another command and the dog returned to excitedly retrieve his treat.

Nobody was hurt, and even though we knew the dog was trained and his trainer was right there with us, there was an undeniable sense of fear at the sheer power of this animal. The ability that this dog had was anything but tame. It was powerful. Good, but powerful.

And God is significantly more powerful than a German Shepherd or a lion. He's God. He is all-knowing, all-present, all-loving, and so much more. It's only natural that we would and should feel an intense fear when in His presence.

So, before you follow in my footsteps by begging God to let you feel Him, understand that the most common emotional reaction to being in God's presence isn't warm fuzzies. It is fear. An appropriate fear of the sheer power of a divine, holy God.

. . . .

One of the questions we have to ask ourselves when we're questioning God and His presence is what we really want from Him. If your answer can be boiled down to "I want to feel good," then maybe God isn't what you're really looking for. Because when God shows up, He just might challenge you to grow in a way that isn't pleasant for you. He might want you to come clean with some sin that will be painful to uproot. He might want you to grow in a way that isn't exactly comfortable.

Think carefully about the cost of God showing up in your life and the resulting emotions. Many times it's positive and wonderful. But it can also be painful, challenging, and uncomfortable. Everything God does in our lives is to draw us closer to Him and make us more into the person He made us to be. But that doesn't mean it will feel good. In fact, growth almost always comes with pain. But we have to learn how to trust God to know what's best for us, even if it isn't always pleasant.

And to those of you praying to feel God, know that God might say no, simply because it's not what's best for you right now.

In 2014, Linds, Eva and I moved from Northern Illinois

to Phoenix, Arizona. When we first moved there, I had to teach Eva, who was about two years old at the time, about avoiding snakes. Until that point, the only time she'd seen snakes was at the zoo, where she would make a point to kiss the glass and say "hi" to them. Had she been attending Hogwarts, she definitely would have been in Slytherin House.

Here's her bonding with a boa contrictor at the zoo when she was only a year and a half old.

HUGE SNAKE

ADORABLE TODDLER

A little girl kissing a snake at the zoo when there's four inches of protective glass between them is pretty adorable. But since we were going to be living in the desert, and since snakes also live in the desert, I realized I should probably teach her about the potential dangers of these reptiles, which I did.

Almost every time I was outside with Eva, I was reminded of a story I heard from Craig Groeschel, founder and senior pastor of Life Church. The story was about when they were in a desert climate and when, one day, he heard his son talking to someone outside. When Craig went out to investigate, he discovered his son talking to a snake.

Groeschel noted that his son *thought* the snake was his friend, even though it wasn't. It was downright dangerous. He compared it to a Bible passage where Jesus was teaching about prayer:

Jesus is teaching about prayer and says: *"You fathers—if your children ask for a fish, do you give them a snake instead? Or if they ask for an egg, do you give them a scorpion? Of course not! So if you sinful people know how to give good gifts to your children, how much more will your heavenly Father give the Holy Spirit to those who ask him."*
– Luke 11:11-13

Sometimes we think we're asking for a fish or an egg, but what we're really asking for is the snake. Sometimes we might be asking God for something we think we need, only He knows it's something dangerous to us.

For example, we might desperately ask God for a boyfriend or girlfriend, but God knows that if we were dating the person we wanted to be dating, it would end up causing us to fall into some deep sin and cause damage to a lot of people. Instead, He chooses to not answer the prayer until we grow a little more and eventually end up in a place where we are healthier and can date more wisely.

Or we might be asking God for success in a particular field of work such as wanting to be a professional athlete, but God knows that success in that field would result in a corruption of our morals through the gain of power or money or both.

Sometimes we think we know what we need, but God knows better. We think we're asking for something good, but we're asking for a snake. So God says "no" or "wait." **We get mad that God isn't answering our prayers, but in truth, God is just being a good Father by not giving us something that could hurt us.**

I'm not saying that asking God to reveal His presence so we can feel Him is a bad thing. Ask Him for it! But we need to understand that God might have an amazing reason for *not* answering us in the way or time that we want Him to.

But regardless of what you pray for, know that God has your best interest in mind, whether that means feeling Him or not.

Psalm 46:10 says, "Be still and know that I am God."

We tend to think that "being still" means pausing for a second, like that pause in a dance song right before the beat drops (special thanks to "Gangnam Style" and every Dubstep song ever). So when it comes to listening to God, we think that a thirty-second pause while cooking our Pop Tart is plenty of time for us to hear all that God is saying to us.

But being still isn't just an absence of activity or a momentary pause in talking. Being still is an attitude. It's a lifestyle.

The Hebrew word for "still" in Psalm 46:10 basically means to "relax." Don't try so hard.

My favorite part about Psalms 46:10 is that it doesn't say, "Be still and then I'll do what you want" or "Be still and then tell me everything you need" or "Be still and then you'll hear/see/feel me immediately."

He says, "Be still and *know*."

Being still isn't a means to an end of getting what we want or think we need. Being still is simply living in an awareness of God's constant presence around us, especially when we can't feel Him.

Trusting in the truth over what we feel is not easy. It can actually be downright terrifying. Because knowing and believing are two different things.

It's one thing to read that God is always present, but to trust in it during a deeply painful moment is much more difficult. You can know something, but believing it is something else entirely.

. . . .

I have one sibling, a younger sister named Breeze. Yes, that's her real name. The story goes that when my dad would drive to work each day, he would pass a street sign named "Gentle Breeze." He came home one day and told my mom, "If we ever have a girl, let's name her Breeze." So they did.

(In case you're wondering, yes my friends and I did try to steal the "Gentle Breeze" street sign when we were in high school as a birthday present for my sister, but we couldn't detach it. I got her a CD instead.)

When Breeze turned twenty-five, she decided to go skydiving for her birthday, and invited her family and friends to join her.

We drove to a skydiving facility in the middle of Wisconsin and signed about four hundred and fifty waivers, watched a safety video (which was also skydiving propaganda to get us to pay a hundred bucks for a video of our experience), and got fitted for equipment. Then they pitched the video package again, and after we declined and they subtly and non-so-subtly pitched it a few dozen more times (I'm proud to say we didn't cave), it was time to go.

My sister, her boyfriend, my best friend, and I all got our gear on and headed out to the airplane hangar to wait for our plane. The adrenaline kept building as we were waiting, and we were all pretty amped up, laughing and talking. We waved to our mom and friends who were going to watch us from the ground. Then our plane rolled up and we got in.

We started heading up to ten thousand feet for our jump. We were all talking and pointing at the various things that looked funny from high up, all the while getting more excited about what was coming.

That whole time, I wasn't really nervous. Skydiving was something I'd wanted to do for years, and I'd seen people do it on TV. Plus I'd heard stories from my friends and they all loved it. I'd watched a safety video and spent the last few hours learning about and getting fit for all the equipment, which was all expensive, proven, and approved by professionals.

We reached the right altitude, the plane leveled off, and I wasn't scared at all...

Until they opened the door of the airplane.

Then, all of a sudden, I was terrified.

I mean, sure, I had been excited and mentally prepared and had all the right knowledge and all the necessary equipment. But *knowing* it was going to be okay and *believing* it was going to be okay was suddenly a very important distinction for me.

I stood there, looking out that door at the earth thousands of feet below, knowing I was going to purposely leave the safety of an airplane to jump out into the safety of…air!?

Everything in my body recoiled. *Wait, what?! What are we doing?!* All my natural instincts to, you know, STAY ALIVE were suddenly setting off all the internal alarms, trying to convince my brain that this was not okay, that a human being is not meant to leap into thin air, and that I should step back into the airplane as quickly as possible.

My survival instinct had to be thinking, *Wait a second— I have to kick in to tell you not to jump out of a freaking airplane? Shouldn't that be sort of an obvious thing that you could figure out on your own?*

With this all raging in my head, and with my heart beating so hard that I'm sure Will.i.am could have sampled it for his next song, I stepped to the edge of the plane.

Below me was nothing. Just space. Just air.

I knew the parachute would save me. I knew the guy strapped to me would deploy it. I knew it would be okay.

But now I had to believe it.

The guy only inches behind my ear yelled that I had to jump out as far as I could on the count of three.

Crap.

"One!..Two!..Three!...JUMP!"

And I did.

And.

It.

Was.

Awesome!

It was such a rush to be moving so quickly through the air, seeing the clouds all around me, and watching planet Earth below me. I looked up to see the rapidly shrinking airplane and the tiny dots of my sister and friends in the air above and below, all of us free-falling to the earth at the same time. It was a major adrenaline kick.

Obviously, since I'm writing this now, I didn't die. The parachute opened, and my guide landed us perfectly on the ground. My pants got grass stains, which I suppose is a small price to pay for staying alive.

You can know you're wearing a parachute, but trusting it's going to open is something else entirely.

Here's us, pre-jump

In the same way, you can know God is with you, but believing it when it doesn't feel like it is much more difficult.

But here's the thing: It is totally worth it.

Having the faith to believe the truth despite what you feel is difficult. It goes against everything culture teaches us. But it is worth it.

What if I had changed my mind when the plane door opened? I could have said, "Forget all the research and preparation that I put into this. Forget the decision I made when I was standing with my feet on the ground. Now that

I'm up here, I'm scared! And do I really know that my parachute will open? Can I be absolutely guaranteed that nothing will go wrong and that everything is okay? No! Forget it! I'm not jumping."

If I had allowed my emotions and doubts to make that choice for me, I would have missed an incredible, amazing, unbelievable experience. No, I didn't have any concrete guarantee that everything was going to be okay. But I had enough assurance to trust that it would be, and as for that small remaining amount of risk? Some jumps in life are worth the risk.

Learning to live every day in a relationship with God, no matter what we feel, is an incredible way to live. It's a bigger, more expansive life than any of you could create for yourself apart from Him.

Mid-jump

Post-jump

It's worth the jump.

The first leap can be scary, but eventually you will get more and more confident in the truth that God is with you. He's with you when life is great and when it's painful. He's with you when the door to that plane opens and everything inside of you revolts and questions. When you choose to believe even when your emotions try to sway you, and as you fall into the wonder and amazement and adventure of life, God will be with you the whole way through. Even though you might get a few grass stains, the exhileration will be worth it.

CHAPTER TEN

OWNERSHIP

Back in the first chapter, I talked about how my Christian faith was very "situational." I was only growing spiritually because of the things around me, like a redwood tree connected to other roots.

In looking back through the very difficult season of not feeling God, one of the biggest ways that I grew was learning how to *own my faith.*

When I could feel God and was surrounded by all things Christian, I didn't have to work very hard to experience God's presence. He was literally in everything and everybody around me. The water just came to me, without any effort of my own.

But once I stopped feeling Him and learned that God was hiding His presence in order to speak to me, I began this journey of learning how to intentionally seek after God and listen for His voice.

It was a totally new experience for me. Now I was learning what it meant to take an active step toward God—by listening to Him, talking to Him, and trusting in the truth instead of my emotions.

And by doing this, I slowly started understanding that I could actually pursue God, not just wait for Him to show up in my life.

It made me think of the phrase, "Christianity is not a religion, it's a relationship." I'd heard that a bunch of times before, but for the first time, I started to understand it.

Any good relationship with a friend, parent, boyfriend, girlfriend, or imaginary friend is going to require effort from both people. If the relationship is going to grow, both have to put some effort into moving towards the other. Any healthy relationship is a two-way street.

Maybe you've been in relationships where you were always the one calling, texting, asking to hang out, asking how they're doing, asking how their life is, but never getting anything back from them. One-way friendships like that are pretty lousy. You begin to feel hurt or angry that you're giving so much and receiving anything in return.

When we think of God, part of what comes to mind is His unconditional love. So sometimes we can get lazy in our relationship with Him because we think, *Well, I know He'll be there when I want or need Him, right?* And while that's true, God doesn't want to love us like a distant aunt that lives in some random part of Louisiana, who you can always count on to send you ten dollars for your birthday even if you haven't talked to her all year. God wants to *know* us.

In our society, we tend to think of the word "know" as being about data. We "know" things like our address or the content of an upcoming test or every funny line from the movie *Paul Blart: Mall Cop*. But in the Bible, the word "know" was much more personal and intimate.

Psalm 139 says:

*O Lord, you have examined my heart
    and know everything about me.
You know when I sit down or stand up.
    You know my thoughts even when I'm far away.
You see me when I travel
    and when I rest at home.
    You know everything I do.
You know what I am going to say
    even before I say it, Lord.*
    – Psalm 139:1-4

The Hebrew word for "know" is the word *yada*, pronounced like a Swedish person saying *yea* and the "a" sound in the word *dad*.

The meanings of yada include "to be acquainted with," "to learn to know," and "to know by experience."

Knowing in the Bible isn't about simply hearing facts or data and then trying to remember them. Knowing is about spending time with someone, experiencing things together, and being together. And through it all, *knowing* them. Not just knowing data about them, but knowing them as a person.

. . . .

I remember when I first met my friend Andy. We hit it off immediately. Within sixty seconds of being introduced, I knew we were gonna be great friends. We had a similar sense of humor, he was genuine, and we had a lot of the same interests, such as golf, music, and ministry. We spent most of that summer together. It was like some cheesy romantic comedy, except way more manly and with more golf.

But there was a definite difference between me knowing things about Andy and actually getting to *know* Andy.

In our first conversations, I learned where he went to school, that he was in an improv comedy group, and that his dad was a pastor. He learned that I played golf, lived in a house with two roommates, and had a dog named Dasher. We were learning about each other, but we still didn't really know each other.

That didn't happen until a few weeks later when I started to learn what Andy was passionate about, what he wanted to do as a career, and who some of his best friends were. Also, he started to know me. He learned how I acted when I was stressed, what excited me about being a youth pastor, and what kind of music I liked to listen to while working.

These weren't just facts or data we were learning. We were actually getting to know each other and were becoming friends.

When it comes to our relationship with God, we could study all the data and facts we want. We could memorize the whole Bible and how many times the book of Acts has the word "the" in it. We could do all that, but still miss what it means to truly know God. To be in a relationship with Him. To open ourselves up for Him to know us further (Psalm 139:23) as we get to know Him further (Psalm 63:1).

Only then will we start to know what His voice sounds like, what it feels like when the Holy Spirit prompts us or speaks to us, how to trust in His love when life is difficult, and so much more.

This is knowing God.

And this is what I learned through my journey of not feeling Him.

Ten years after making a decision to accept Jesus' forgiveness for my sins, I finally was beginning to understand how to own my faith.

To seek after God instead of just wait for Him.

To listen for His voice instead of just talking at Him.

To trust His love and presence when I didn't feel it.

To obey His promptings and step out of my comfort zone.

I was figuring out how to seek after God and take part in our relationship. To actually have a relationship.

After all, hide and seek is only fun when you take turns hiding and seeking. I'd been hiding (more like being lazy) for a bunch of years, and now it was my turn to do the finding.

The purpose of our life on earth is to grow closer in our relationship with God and to be with Him more, so that once our physical bodies die, our true desire is to be with God forever. Those who would rather not be with God for eternity will go to what we call hell, which is eternal separation from God. The Christian author and theologian, Dallas Willard once said, "I'm quite sure that God will allow everyone into heaven that can possibly stand it." Meaning that anyone who desires to spend eternity with God will be able to!

Not being able to feel or sense God with me was a difficult season, and I'm sure there will be seasons when I experience it again. But I am so happy to have learned (among many other things) what it means to own my faith and seek after God on my own. My life and faith will never be the same as I continue to learn every single day how to pursue God more, to know Him more, and be known by Him.

Knowing God is with us is sometimes a choice, not an assumption. Sometimes we won't feel Him, but we choose to believe, to know that He is there.

Because God promises that He will never, ever leave us.

Yea, though I walk through the valley of the shadow of death, I will fear no evil; For You are with me...
– Psalm 23:4

And when we can't feel God, we can still seek Him, and still find Him.

Because He is there, and He is speaking. He wants us to seek Him so we will find Him. Maybe not in the way we want or expect to, but we will. We will find His voice. Find His His peace. Find His joy.

He is there.

Ask God to show Himself to you.

Jeremiah 29:13 says, "If you look for me wholeheartely, you will find me." What God doesn't say is when we will find Him or by what method of seeking. We will find God when we seek Him. It might not be where or how or, especially, when we expect. But we will find Him. That's the process of seeking, after all. Looking for something, not knowing where it will be found, but knowing it is there for the discovery.

That's why the Bible has verses like this:

I will wait for the Lord,
*   who has turned away from the descendants of Jacob.*
I will put my hope in him.
    – Isaiah 8:17

We sometimes have to wait for God. Not because He's too busy for us or too far away and there's bad traffic, but because His timing is perfect and sometimes there's a reason He doesn't want us to feel Him.

In the words of hip-hop artist Lecrae, "God is never late, we're just impatient."

But even when we can't feel Him, we can *know* Him. We can seek after Him. And when we do, God promises that we will find Him. We might not feel Him, but He is there.

God's silence is not His absence. The truth remains: you are never alone!!!

CHAPTER ELEVEN

EVA

When my daughter Eva was born, I was so excited to be a dad. I couldn't wait. I had been not-so-secretly hoping that our first child would be a girl, and I was ready to be the best dad I could be to her.

As Linds and I were preparing to be parents, I had heard that often times, dads have trouble connecting with their newborn kids until they are about a year old. I thought that was bogus. I thought, *No way! I'm totally going to connect with my little girl from the very beginning! She's going to be daddy's little girl and we're gonna hang out and have this awesome connection from the second she's born!*

And I'm proud to say that I was totally and completely... wrong.

It took a little while for me to feel connected to Eva.

Not that I didn't love her. In fact, I was shocked at how much I *DID* love her, despite the fact that we weren't experiencing an intense bond. All she did was eat, sleep, and poop (sometimes all at the same time), but I kept looking at this little lump of a person and thinking, *I really like you. I don't know why, but I'm crazy about you.*

One day, when she was about six months old, I was home alone with her and I needed to do something. When babies are that young, they can't do much more than lie on their backs, flailing their limbs around like helpless ladybugs. Eva couldn't roll over, so I figured I'd set her in the middle of our king-sized bed while I got done what I needed to do in the next room.

And you might be anticipating where I'm going with this, but no, she didn't fall off the bed onto my broken glass collection or something. Also I don't have a broken glass collection.

I was only about five feet away from her, but because of the way our house was set up, I was blocked from her view.

After a few seconds, she began to cry. But at this point, I was already involved in what I was doing and wasn't able to step away, so all I could do was talk to her.

I called to her and said, "It's okay, Eva. I'm right here, baby, I'll be right there in a minute."

I peeked around the corner to make sure she was okay.

And the second she heard my voice, she stopped crying and looked around.

Then after a few more seconds, when she didn't see me, she started crying again.

I called to her again, "Eva, honey, I love you and am right here. I'll come get you in just a second. Hang on, baby."

She stopped crying and listened again. So I decided to keep talking to her from the other room.

After another minute or so, I returned to the bedroom. As I scooped her into my arms, I distinctly remember God saying to me, *Dugan, sometimes that's what I do with you. Sometimes I'm right next to you and you won't be able to see me, but you will be able to hear me.*

The power of the moment slammed into my heart as God spoke that truth to me. He is here. He is with me. Always. And He is with you. He is speaking. While we might want to cry and scream and shout and complain, sometimes we need to trust and listen.

Because once we do, we'll hear His voice saying, *I'm right here. I know you can't see me but I'm here. I love you so much, and soon you'll feel me wrap my arms around you. But until then, don't worry. You're not alone.*

WHEN DARKNESS SEEMS TO HIDE HIS FACE
I REST ON HIS UNCHANGING GRACE
IN EVERY HIGH AND STORMY GALE
MY ANCHOR HOLDS WITHIN THE VEIL

———————

Cornerstone, by Hillsong

WHAT ABOUT TODAY?

As I write this, it's 2015 and I'm thirty years old. Most of what's written in this book happened to me more than ten years ago, and you might be wondering, *What about since then?*

The truth is that it's been a journey. There wasn't a moment when all of a sudden a switch was flipped and I felt God like the "good old days." I've had to continually learn how to follow God both when I feel Him and when I don't. So if you were hoping I'd say something like, "After not feeling God, he taught me some stuff and now I feel Him more every day!" I'm sorry, but that's not how it's been.

There have been moments and seasons when I've felt God's presence again in powerful ways—when praying by myself, when talking with a friend, hearing someone's story, or even in a fight with my wife. But I am still discovering more about following God, not the emotion of Him.

And the vast majority of my relationship with God has grown regardless of the emotions I've felt, rather than because of them.

I am grateful for this. Had I not learned the truth of God's presence and how to hear His voice without feeling His presence, I know that our relationship would not be where it is today. I'm so grateful to God for hiding Himself from me so that he could teach me the discipline of seeking and knowing Him. Through it, I've discovered how to embrace God as a constant, solid foundation of my life.

The Bible sometimes describes God as a "rock" (Genesis 49:24, Psalm 18:2, 2 Samuel 22:3, Isaiah 28:16, Mark 12:10). There are two main Hebrew words used in the Old Testament that are translated to mean "rock" or "stone." One of these words is Eben (sounds like *evan*), which can be translated as "motionless."

The Bible tells us that God is motionless. That He doesn't move. When our lives are in turmoil and the storm is raging around us, when our emotions are on a roller coaster going up and down, when there's nothing else to hold on to, God is right there. Motionless. Still.

All we have to do to "be still" (Psalm 46:10) is be with God. Because He doesn't move.

So if you're on a journey of figuring out what it means to follow God even when you don't feel His presence, you are learning an incredibly powerful truth that God is with you no matter what. You are learning how to truly walk by faith and trust in God and His truth, not what you see or feel.

And through this, you will begin a relationship with God that will become the foundation of everything you are. The foundation of your thoughts and actions and decisions and relationships and future. A God who is always there, always speaking, and motionless.

I pray that you will place both feet firmly on the motionless Rock and live the rest of your days in awareness of God's presence and the truth that He is with you, always.

Thanks for reading.

February, 2015

A NOTE TO LEADERS
ABOUT STUDENT MINISTRIES

I didn't want to conclude this book without addressing a few additional thoughts, specifically based on the content in Chapter 2.

After researching the way our brains develop and the impact an emotionally tailored student ministry can have on the young mind, the question then becomes this: How do student ministries operate to avoid setting students up with false emotional expectations of their relationship with God?

My answer: *Carefully.*

The emotions of teenagers are fragile and sensitive. Much like you would handle a stick of dynamite or a glass of milk that's way too full, student ministries need to approach students' emotions with intentionality and caution. When thinking through a retreat, camp, teaching, worship, video, or small group curriculum, there needs to be a direct focus on how it will be filtered through the emotional mind of a student. Will it set them up for truth and a healthy perspective of God? Or will it build a foundation of their faith on an emotion?

When God's presence is obvious and there's a powerful emotional experience, address it! Celebrate it! But also make it very clear to students that the emotion of God's presence isn't the goal, nor is it a healthy expectation for their faith. It's an amazing plus, but not the focus.

When talking about making a decision to follow Christ, take the emotion out of it! Speak truth to students, not emotion. A student's brain is already not set up to fully process emotional responses like the adult brain. This can make them prone to making emotional decisions. This is especially true with any kind of reward incentive they might see a part of Christianity when salvation is presented in a Jesus-will-make-everything-perfect kind of way.

God is not a fix-it-all product that is there to make us feel better. There's a difference between saying "God will bless you with hope, peace, and joy!" versus saying or implying "God can make you feel happy all the time!" The fact that we can put our hope in God, experience peace that passes understanding, and have joy despite trials is not an emotional truth, but a supernatural one.

When these kinds of Biblical principals are too-closely

associated with emotion, it can cause students to associate their salvation through Jesus and decision to surrender to Him on that reward. This means that when they feel hopeless, anxious, or depressed, their assumption is that God is not with them, or that He's not fixing their problems like He should.

Celebrate emotion, but don't build your foundation on it. Be very clear to students that following Jesus is often times emotion-less…and that's totally okay! Students need their leaders and pastors to address the power of following Jesus in spite of our emotions, not because of them. They also need to learn about how to process emotion in a healthy way, one that is a challenge for their developing brain.

By doing that, we are setting them up for a healthier faith, rooted in truth and then enhanced by emotion. Students will then learn how to seek after God, not just the sensation of Him.

And by doing that, their faith can be better sustained after high school, after college, and in the moments in life when God feels farthest away. Because they will know that their emotion doesn't determine God's presence. God is always with them and God is speaking to them.

Here are some practical thoughts on what I believe student ministries should focus on:

- **Don't try to manufacture an emotional moment.**

I know in our world of Coldplay songs and slow motion video, this is tough to consider. When it comes to the gospel and the life-changing power of God in our every day lives, we can be so tempted to want to play to students' emotion because we know that it will evoke a response. But while that response might feel like a victory in the moment, it is more likely giving them an emotional response that they can't logically process through. Not only that, but the intensity of their emotion also risks connecting them with God through their emotion, rather than experiencing a positive emotion because they connected with God.

• **Make a point to talk about the reality, power, and joy of following God outside of having an emotional experience.** Many times, after a retreat-type experience, the message to students is, "Everything you experienced here at camp/on this missions trip/at this youth event—this can be part of your every day life. Go home on fire for the Lord and don't lose the flame. This shouldn't be a once-a-year occasion but a way of every day living."

A healthier version might be, "These experiences that you've had—remember them. Remember what God spoke to you. Remember the moments that you felt His presence and knew He was close. But being a disciple of Christ doesn't mean living in a constant state of emotional connectedness with God and your friends. It's a day in, day out decision to follow Jesus regardless your circumstances and despite your emotions. So don't be alarmed in a week if you feel differently than you feel at this very moment. That doesn't mean that this moment isn't a legitimate experience with God, it just means that, like in any relationship, all of your moments with God aren't going to feel this way."

• **Teach healthy emotion.** Make sure to not teach that emotions are bad or wrong. Because they're not. They're a wonderful gift from God. However, they are not a strong foundation for important things in life, like faith or relationships or buying a new car. Present the word of God as truth. It doesn't need to be wrapped in emotion to impact students' lives.

One of the best ways to teach healthy emotions is by focusing on telling personal stories. I believe this is the best form of raw emotion for students to see, as it relates to encounters with God. Personal testimony can teach healthy emotion as it relates to God's movement in our lives.

I hope this helps. I'm still learning myself by seeking God and other wise student leaders on how to best help students have an authentic encounter with the living God, while also building their faith on a solid foundation.

I pray you are challenged and inspired. I pray that you will go and teach truth. Truth that trumps emotion.

February, 2015

Linds – For all your patience, encouragement, and wisdom as I wrote this. Also for your hotness.

Steve – Mostly for your friendship but also for your mad editing skills. This book wouldn't be close to anything good without having been filtered through your discernment and wisdom.

Joy – For being the kind of friend who can speak wisdom into my life with record speed. Thanks for your love and your wonderful editing chops.

Nashville – For all your various coffee shops that housed me while I wrote. Sorry I lost your respect by adding sugar to it. Please still accept me since I wear flannel and sometimes have a ponytail.

Mom – For all the days you spent time loving and pouring into our daughter so I could write.

Annie – For your advice that enabled me to learn from your experience. Like a way cooler version of me from the future.

90's music – For being the soundtrack to my writing.

Assassin's Creed – For providing a much-needed mental break after long periods of writing.

Cereal.

SOURCES

Graham Cooke, Hiddenness & Manifestation: What is Really Happening When God Doesn't Seem to be Present? Vacaville, CA: Brilliant Book House, 2003.

Ney Bailey, Faith is Not a Feeling: Choosing to Take God at His Word. Colorado Springs, CO: WaterBrook Press, 2002.

Shannon Brownlee, "Inside the Teen Brain." U.S. News & World Report: Aug 9, 1999

Deborah Yurgelun-Todd, "Inside the Teenage Brain." PBS Frontline.

Derek Melleby, "Why Students Abandon Their Faith: Lessons From William Wilberforce." The Center for Parent/Youth Understanding, 2008.

John Stonestreet and Chuck Edwards, "Students Abandoning Their Faith: What Happens and What We Can Do." Summit Ministries.

DISCUSSION QUESTIONS

CHAPTER 1

— What do you hate most about being alone?

— What's a time when you wanted to feel God but didn't?

— Have you ever wondered if God left you?

— What did you think it meant when you couldn't feel God?

CHAPTER 2

— Why do you think we put so much importance on our emotions and what we feel?

— Have you ever felt alone even though you were surrounded by people?

— Has there been a time when you've chased after the feeling of God more than God Himself?

— Knowing a little more about how our brain works, what do you think is the best way to process emotion?

CHAPTER 3

— As you read the account of Emmaus in Luke 24, what do you think the attitude of the disciples was like? What about Jesus'?

— Based on Jacob in Genesis 28, can you think of a time when God was with you but you were not aware of it?

— Have you ever considered that even Jesus didn't feel God at times He wanted to (while praying in the garden, on the cross etc.)? What does that tell you about the character of Jesus?

CHAPTER 4

— What is a time in your life when you were hiding from God (intentionally or not) and God found you?

— Have you ever searched for God? Why or why not? How did you search for Him? Did you find Him?

— When is a time when God's presence was "manifested" in your life? When is a time when you felt like God was "hidden" from you?

CHAPTER 5

— What does it make you think when you read in Luke 24 that God was the One who kept the disciples from knowing it was Jesus who was with them?

— Do you think God has or is preventing you from feeling Him?

— If so, have you ever taken the time and practice to quiet yourself and listen for His voice?

CHAPTER 6

— Can you think of a time when you heard God speak to you?

— Why do you think God's voice is a whisper?

— What do you think is a time and place for you to practice the six steps of listening to God?

CHAPTER 7

— What's a time when you (or someone you were with) felt an emotion that was "wrong"?

— Which piece of evidence from the Bible jumped out at you the most?

— At what point during Joseph's life do you think it was most difficult for him to trust God was still with him?

CHAPTER 8

— Have you ever been brutally honest with God about what you're feeling (or not feeling)?

— What is a time that you clearly remember seeing, feeling, hearing, or sensing God?

— How will you remind yourself of the truth every day?

CHAPTER 9

— Have you ever felt fear because of something God asked you to do?

— What is something you've been asking God for that He might be saying "no" to because it would be dangerous for you?

— Do you truly want God in your life? Or do you just want Him to make you feel good?

CHAPTER 10

— Have you owned your faith and sought after God? Or does it just grow because of the thing and people around you?

— Do you truly know (yada) God? Have you let Him know you?

— What is one way you need to actively seek after God more?

ABOUT THE AUTHOR

Part comedian, part teacher, and part pastor, Dugan is
a traveling speaker who loves to serve any event geared
towards middle school, high school, or college students.
He lives in Madison, Wisconsin with his wife, Lindsay
and daughter, Eva.

If you're interested in having Dugan come speak at your
next retreat, camp, conference, ministry night or leader
training, head to dugansherbondy.com (where you can also
download a free copy of Dugan's book, *Sow What?: The
Sometimes Unfruitful Work of Student Ministries…
And How it Changes Lives*) or send an e-mail to
duganEsherbondy@gmail.com.